By patriarchy I mean a culture that is slanted so that men are valued a lot and women are valued less; or in which men's prestige is up and women's prestige is down.

A conceptual trap is to the thought world of the mind what the astronomers' black holes are to the universe. Once inside, there seems to be no way of getting out or seeing out. A conceptual trap is a way of thinking which is like a room that, once you are inside, you cannot imagine a world outside.

Reality has always been a seamless web of interrelated systems. Within patriarchy we have simply tried to superimpose our humanly generated hierarchical paradigms onto that reality in much the same way that we projected in earlier times a pre-Copernican astronomy upon the skies.

AUTHOR OF—

Green Paradise Lost:
formerly *Why the Green Nigger?*
(1979, 1982)

The Energy Oratorio
(1978)

CO-AUTHOR (with David Dodson Gray)—

Children of Joy:
Raising Your Own Home-Grown Christians
(1975)

CO-AUTHOR—
(with David Dodson Gray & William F. Martin)

Growth and Its Implications for the Future:
A Report Prepared for Congressional Hearings
(1974, 1975)

PATRIARCHY
as a
CONCEPTUAL
TRAP

ELIZABETH DODSON GRAY

Roundtable Press
WELLESLEY, MASSACHUSETTS

Every effort has been made to obtain permission to reprint cartoons.
In one instance the artist could not be located nor could the place of original
publication be identified; permission is still sought and the artist is asked to
communicate with the author.

Portions of this book appeared in abridged form under the same title in
Alternative Futures: The Journal of Utopian Studies,
4.2–3 (Spring/Summer 1981): 135–155.
Portions of chapter 3 appeared in *Making It Happen: A Positive Guide to the
Future,* ed. John M. Richardson, Jr. (Washington, DC: US Association for The
Club of Rome, 1982).

Biblical quotations from the Revised Standard Version of the Bible—
copyright © 1946, 1952, 1971, 1973 by the Division of Christian Education
of the National Council of Churches of Christ in the USA
—are used by permission.

Book design by Elizabeth and David Dodson Gray
Printed in the United States of America at Nimrod Press, Boston, MA.

Library of Congress Catalog Card Number: 82-60729
ISBN 0-934512-04-3

*To my colleagues
in the U.S. Association for The Club of Rome—
who have been a nurturing environment
for my thinking on these matters;*

and—

*to my husband David
who has never confused
my ability to critique male culture
with my ability to love him.*

Contents

3.

4.

5.

6.

"I still say there are no limits to growth."

About Conceptual Traps

By Thomas W. Wilson, Jr.

Our World-Future

There has been a remarkable increase in public awareness of the global predicament since *The Limits to
Growth* first appeared in 1972. This awareness has been
fed by a series of subsequent world models, by a scatter-
ing of national associations affiliated with The Club of
Rome, by the 1972 UN Conference on the Human Environment, and by the emergence of something loosely
known as the "futurist movement." And yes, there also
has been a backlash against "gloom and doom."

Our compound global predicament normally is described in terms of its major component parts:
- population growth,
- pressures on natural resources and systems,
- energy shortages,
- pollution,
- threatened species,
- human impacts on climate and ecosystems, and
- capital requirements.

At the option of whoever is doing the describing, factors
such as malnutrition, inflation, unemployment, and
other contemporary ills may be added to this list. The
founder of The Club of Rome, Aurelio Peccei, usually
mentions nuclear weapons, although most globalists and
futurists seem to believe that nuclear war is for somebody
else to worry about.

The Smoothness of Our Predicament

The very wholeness of the Future Problem leaves the impression that it is round and smooth with no apparent handles to get hold of. There are no obvious places to start remedial action which have emerged. And no obvious strategies have been evolved, except to work away at some component, vaguely aware that this could so compound another piece of the problem as to be counterproductive.

Thus there is difficulty in getting much beyond an initial awareness and an ideological stand-off regarding all these interconnected global problems we face. And that difficulty has been aggravated by professional specialization, by the sharply defined focus of academic disciplines, by inherited patterns of organizations and functions, and by sectoral expertise dealing with some part of the overall problem. All these have mitigated against integrated analysis by public and private institutions involved in governance.

Somehow we must rescue the perception that there actually is a global predicament from such technical analysis and its quantification in economic terms. This is an important perception, and it must be related to the realm of political action and our current decision-making. We must try to identify and articulate the politics of the present predicament. Perhaps, to begin with, it can be reconceptualized in terms more conducive to political analysis.

The Task of Reconceptualizing

One way to go about reconceptualizing is to look behind the major trends contributing to the global predicament, identify the human behavior patterns that got us into this mess, and then examine, if we can, the dominant beliefs, ideas, and assumptions that influenced the behavior that brought us to where we are today.

It is obvious that this could grow into a vast academic research agenda. But for the sake of argument one might begin with a quick-and-dirty exploration of the following five ideas/attitudes/assumptions:
The assumption that—

• *A major mission of humanity on earth is to conquer nature.*

The assumption that—

• *The best if not the only road to social progress lies in continuous expansion of the gross output of material goods and services on a national and global basis.*

The assumption that—

• *Sooner or later science will provide solutions for social problems;*

and the related assumption that—

• *Accumulating knowledge from application of the scientific method and the rule of reason will abolish emotion and superstition from the political process.*

The assumption that—

• *Because of male superiority, societies are naturally organized along patriarchy lines.*

The assumption that—

• *The main business in international relations is the manipulation of military-based power in support of inherently conflicting national interests, especially those of the "great powers."*

14

"What a beautiful spot to build something!"

Each of these assumptions has influenced millions of decisions at all levels of social organization throughout the Western world during the past few centuries. Whatever merit any of these perceptions may have had in the past, it is evident that they have no basis in contemporary political, social, or strategic realities.

A Set of Conceptual Traps

In this perspective, the present global predicament can be described in terms of a set of outmoded beliefs—or *conceptual traps*[1]—that have influenced endless decisions over a long period of time and have now become part of the global problem. In this perspective, the much-touted but seldom-detailed "transition" we are now in can be seen as a struggle for liberation from a set of malignant mindsets.

It is obvious that this struggle has been going on in this and other countries for the past decade or two. Indeed, the civil rights movement, women's liberation, the environmental movement, conservation, decentralization, family planning, and other familiar social phenomena already have gone far enough to have produced a powerful backlash. It is conceivable that this, in turn, will lead to a synthesis that might resolve the sterile confrontation over the causes and cures of the global predicament.

In any event, I suggest it is by exploring the lively ferment in the field of ideas, beliefs, assumptions, and values—as distinguished from more of the technical analysis—that we can begin to see the political dimensions of the *problematique* and how to steer the political process of adaptation.[2]

1.

Patriarchy

Let's begin with the basics. What is a conceptual trap? And what is patriarchy?

A conceptual trap is to the thought world of the mind what the astronomers' black holes are to the universe. Once inside, there seems to be no way of getting out or seeing out. A conceptual trap is a way of thinking that is like a room which—once inside—you cannot imagine a world outside.

"All the powers that be being present and accounted for, let us begin."

By patriarchy I mean a culture that is slanted so that men are valued a lot and women are valued less; or in which men's prestige is up and women's prestige is down.

"WOMEN INVENT THE CRAZIEST THINGS."

The Pervasiveness of Patriarchy

Margaret Mead said that when she journeyed in her anthropological studies from tribe to tribe she discovered that it did not matter what was done in a particular tribe—it only mattered who did it. If the weaving in a particular tribe was done by men, it was an occupation of high prestige. If twenty miles away weaving was done by women, it was of low prestige. The important thing was which sex did it.[1] Think of cooking in the home—which is not valued. But if someone really does superlative cooking outside the home, it's a chef—and he's male.

It's interesting that Adam Smith thought this way too, as have most subsequent economists. When they speak of labor creating value and about payment for that value, it is very clear the labor they are talking about is not the labor of women in the home. The labor that creates value and is "productive" is industrial labor and in most generations has been the labor of men. The labor of women in bearing and caring for children, for example, was not considered, despite it being absolutely fundamental to an entire economy and culture.

"Actually, I'm waiting for a detergent that sorts and folds."

Around the world it is women who are the basic caregivers of life. It is women who have defined their total existence in terms of meeting basic human needs. It is women in many societies who actually grow the food that is eaten. It is almost invariably women who are cooking that food, serving it, and cleaning the dirty dishes after it is eaten.

And it is women who are bearing and caring for the children, keeping the homes clean and doing the laundry, in addition to nursing the sick and caring for the dying. In culture after culture, women are charged with providing for many, often most, of the basic needs of the human beings around them.

*   *   *

Now I have discovered that when I say things critical of male culture people very quickly say, "You must hate men!" Before I go further I want you to know I've been very happily married to the same man for a quarter-century, and I really don't hate men. I have many good male friends. What I am talking about is not individual men but a male-dominated social system—patriarchy—which is tilted in a particular way.

Who Controls the Myth System?

In my reading of history I find patriarchy everywhere: men (and things men do) have been valued a lot in every place and time, and women (and things women do) have been valued less. That tilt is the essence of patriarchy. Several years ago a group of feminist anthropologists reported in *Woman, Culture, and Society*[2] that every culture they knew was, in their judgment, patriarchal.

When I say patriarchy is pervasive, what I mean is that men are always in control of the myth system. Even in matrilineal societies where descent is counted through women, it is still men who control the myth system. Similarly, in Hinduism the goddesses offer a very favorable portrait of women's sexual energies. Yet Hinduism is still a myth system totally organized from the viewpoint of the male. The decisive question is always, "Who controls the myth system?"—who is in charge of the social and religious construction of reality?

THE RULES OF THE GAME

The Origins of Patriarchy

I think patriarchy has been with us from the beginning. I do not agree with the feminists who assert that we had an early matriarchy which was displaced before recorded history. Elizabeth Janeway in *Between Myth and Morning* is persuasive to me on this point when she considers the numerous little "Venus" statues from the Old Stone Age, which are usually cited as archeological evidence of an earlier and widespread matriarchal culture. These are small statues of a very pregnant woman with full breasts and distended stomach but no face or head.

Janeway asks whether women would represent or "myth" themselves this way if they were in control of the myth system.[3] I don't think they would. I agree with Janeway that the little Venuses are a very early and incredibly appreciative expression of primitive man's view of the fertility of women, with which he was very impressed. So I have not been convinced by Elizabeth Gould Davis' *The First Sex*[4] and Merlin Stone's *When God Was a Woman*.[5]

It is clear there was indeed an overturn of the gods and of the way in which religious symbolization was structured. But my major concern here is to point out that, whatever woman's symbolic *place* may have been in the mythologies and symbol systems of very early fertility religions, I see no evidence that women were ever *in control* of those myths and symbol systems. The earliest mythologies were reverential about female fertility and made women primal in the religious system. In the overturn of the gods,[6] that changed to a symbol system which gave primacy to male fertility. This is what we have inherited.

Judaism—A Male Fertility Cult?

My own graduate training twenty-five years ago was in theology, and my personal commitment is as an inheritor of the Judeo-Christian tradition. Until recently I was insensitive (as was everyone else I knew) to our Judeo-Christian tradition being, in important respects, a male fertility cult. How else can we characterize a religion in which the major cultic ritual by which the mark of the covenant is passed from generation to generation is the circumcision of the male phallus?

Until recently I have also been insensitive to the sociological or anthropological significance of such New Testament accounts as the purification of Mary after the birth of Jesus (Luke 2:22) as well as its antecedents in the religious laws and customs of the Old Testament. In Judaism sacred space was held to be contaminated by women who had been menstruating or had given birth. Before women could be allowed to reenter the sacred worship space, they had to be ritually cleansed after such female blood-centered activities.

These views from Judaism and late antiquity are evident in our present day in the liturgical calendars, prayer books, and recent practices of some Christian churches. The Purification of Mary (February 2) is a feastday in the calendars of liturgical churches still. The Book of Common Prayer (1928) used in the Episcopal Church into the mid-1970s contained a "Service of Thanksgiving for Women after Child-birth," and subtitled "The Churching of Women." Two English women-friends have told me of their experience of giving birth to children during the 1950s, each in different parts of England, and being unwelcome in the homes of relatives and friends until after they had gone to the local clergy and "been churched."

All this is an outgrowth of an ancient view in which female blood contaminates, while male blood and blood-sacrifices are associated with the central acts of atonement, forgiveness and reconciliation—and are perceived as the right and proper holy use of sacred space. In ancient Judaism there were sacrifices of lambs and other animals. In Christian theologies of atonement, the death of Jesus on the cross has been interpreted as a sacrifice in which Jesus was "the Lamb of God that takes away the sins of the world." In the central liturgical action of Christian worship, the service of Holy Communion (or Mass), Jesus' blood-sacrifice is remembered and, in some views, reenacted in the sacred space of church or cathedral, catacomb or home.

When the holy space of a religion is sacred for male sexuality (as in the marking of the covenant upon the male phallus in circumcision), and sacred for blood-sacrifice presided over by males; and when that same holy space is contaminated by female blood and female fertility (as in menstruating and in giving birth), we are dealing with a male fertility cult, no matter what its other lofty spiritual insights may be.

I feel a need at this point to state my own current faith-stance in relation to Judeo-Christianity. I am a child of this tradition. I grew up a Southern Baptist, and I owe my very deep and real relationship to God to that tradition. God has been extraordinarily real and important to me ever since I can remember being myself, which is to say since my earliest childhood. Abraham and Moses, Amos and Hosea, these are my faith forebears. It is in the midst of this tradition that the Creator God has been revealed to me, and I cannot myself move away from its authentic glimpses into God's justice and compassion.

But I must nowadays acknowledge that this deeply felt faith-tradition is flawed by a serious distortion—and that distortion is its patriarchal character or shape. It is a flaw which has distorted its perception and transmission of even its most true insights into ultimate religious reality.

I sometimes say that the best of our Judeo-Christian tradition has worked for us like a telescope or microscope, permitting us to catch glimpses of ultimate religious reality. But its lens has had a crack, a flaw as-it-were in the glass, and this has distorted even the best of its perceptions.

Drawing by Baloo; © 1981 *Good Housekeeping Magazine.*

"First, though, I'd like to read you a little something I wrote myself..."

It is now high time in the history of this always-dynamic and always-changing religious tradition to acknowledge its perceptions and also its distortions as a heritage. It is time for women and men, and most especially for men, to acknowledge the distortions by which patriarchy has literally bent our tradition out of shape—and to repent of that bending. It is now time to unbend those distortions. It is a time to emancipate that holy space which has been sacred for men and male fertility alone, so that it may become a true sacred space not only for all humans but for all to which God gives being.

The Overturn of the Gods

Recent medical discoveries about women's menstruation cast new light for me on this early overturn of the gods. We are now aware that some women who are below a certain level of body fat do not menstruate regularly. In the United States today these are notably women athletes in strenuous training, some serious joggers, and ballet dancers.[7] I can therefore imagine that in the very early nomadic period of human pre-history, when women were part of hunter-gatherer bands constantly on the move and had a sparse diet low in fat except for sporadic feasts from the hunt, why then women could have menstruated very irregularly.

In such a life, even though they might copulate often, they would give birth rarely. In such an existence, women as well as men could for a long time be truly unaware of the males' role in reproduction. Women's fertility, especially if synchronized with each other,[8] would seem almost magical and also totally within the control of women. Even if men were in control of the myth system of that early culture, it would not be strange for the men of that culture to celebrate this seemingly magical female fertility by creating little goddess figures of full breasts and pregnant bellies—the little Venuses.

But later in our human story most humans moved on from being nomadic hunter-gatherers and began settled agriculture. Women, as the gatherers (the men were off hunting), probably played a major role in this discovery of agriculture as well as the domesticating of small animals.[9] They had discovered the nutritional potential of planning the cycles of planting and harvesting, and now that everything did not have to be carried everywhere by the nomadic group, they could store food to eat between harvests. Women as well as men would eat more regularly. The women would put on more body fat and hence begin to menstruate and give birth more regularly.

Men in this new settled agriculture gradually figured out that it was not women by themselves who brought life. Then there was what the archeological evidence clearly suggests was an "overthrow of the gods." The old pantheon of fertility goddesses was superceded by what I see as just another form of religion done from the male point of view, this one now celebrating male gods seen as like them and in their own phallic image.

My major point here is that I do think there was an overturn of the gods, of the way in which the religious symbolization was carried on. But I see no evidence that women were ever in control of the myth systems, either before or after that great shift.

*"I don't believe in it any more either,
but it gives the young people something to hold on to."*

Why Patriarchy Developed

We'll never know for sure why patriarchy developed. My intuition is that this slanted or tilted society was an expression of the males' desire to create a culture to make themselves feel good. Very early I think it seemed to everyone that the male could not do what women could do. Women seemed to be related to the fertility of the soil and to bring new life almost magically out of their bodies. Men were very impressed and, as I've been saying, out of this came the great emphasis upon women's fertility in early mythology and religion. If women could do all this, the question for men must have been—"What could men do that was nearly so impressive?" What men could do— and did do in a kind of massive "reaction-formation"— was to shape a culture to reassure themselves.

"Yes!"

Drawing by Verne Myers;
© 1979 *Good Housekeeping Magazine.*

31

The Shaping of a Culture to Reassure

Feminist anthropologists have pointed out that culture comes from men (and *not* from women).[10]

How did that happen? They have suggested that men had the freedom to go out of the home and create human culture because they were not involved bearing the children, caring for them, feeding them, and all the rest.

I am reminded of Perdita Huston's interviews with women in Kenya and elsewhere in the Third World. It is the women who not only bear the children and care for them but raise all the food as well as preparing it and serving it. Third World women are busy from dawn to dusk simply making the basic necessities of life happen for their families.[11]

Michelle Zimbalist Rosaldo, in her "theoretical overview" to a collection of essays by feminist anthropologists, says—"Put quite simply, men have no single commitment as enduring, time-consuming, and emotionally compelling—as close to seeming necessary and natural—as the relation of a woman to her infant child; and *so men are free to form those broader associations that we call 'society,' universalistic systems of order, meaning and commitment that link particular mother-child groups.*"[12]

We can glimpse all these relationships—mother, children, and the process of males creating a culture—in the biblical account of the virtuous wife in Proverbs 31. Unlike many other passages in the Bible, this passage cannot be dated precisely by the style of its language. It could have been written any time from 1000 BC to 400 BC, I am told by a biblical scholar. The passage describes the life of ordinary people, which did not change that much through those years no matter who occupied the throne.

A good wife who can find?
　She is far more precious than jewels....
She seeks wool and flax,
　and works with willing hands.
She is like the ships of the merchant,
　she brings her food from afar.
She rises while it is yet night
　and provides food for her household
　and tasks for her maidens.
She considers a field and buys it;
　with the fruit of her hands she plants a vineyard.
She girds her loins with strength
　and makes her arms strong.
She perceives that her merchandise is profitable.
　Her lamp does not go out at night.
She puts her hands to the distaff,.
She opens her hands to the poor,
　and reaches out her hands to the needy....
She looks well to the ways of her household,
　and does not eat the bread of idleness.

Now what of the role of the male in that world? "Her husband is known in the gates,/ when he sits among the elders of the land" (Prov. 31:23). My biblical colleague tells me that the men's responsibilities were to wage war, and to be the primary legal figures, for law was made at the city gates where people gathered as they passed in and out. It was here that men (in Rosaldo's terms) "form those broader associations that we call 'society'."

We find an extended anecdotal account of one such transaction at the gate in Ruth 4:1–12. The account has been preserved because it is about the great-grandmother of the greatest biblical king, David. It is about how, following the death of her first husband, Ruth came to a kinsman, Boaz, while he slept and asked him to provide her with offspring. He refused to until she became his wife. So he bought Ruth in connection with his taking title to a parcel of land that had belonged to her deceased husband. This legal transaction was made and confirmed by Boaz at the gate of the city in the presence of the elders. It is clear that the law was being made and transacted at the gates where the men gathered and talked—and that they were the only "powers that be" in such matters.

Thus, in the Third World today, we see women working while men are in charge of the culture. In biblical times we see women working and men making the law at the gates. Can we see further back, even to primate times, and are there interesting primate precursors to these early human patterns? Descriptive field studies with primates during the 1960s and 1970s suggest that indeed there are.

Evelyn Reed, writing about "Primatology and Prejudice,"[13] examined the primatology literature and reports that the cohesive group consists of the female and the offspring. In contrast with these more enduring relations between females and their young, the relations between adult males and females are ephemeral.[14] According to Washburn and DeVore "sexual pairing is incidental in the life of a female primate and usually short-lived."[15]

"Thus, the 'grouping pattern' of primates is not based upon the ephemeral sexual relations between males and females, but upon the more durable bonds of females and offspring. *The animal 'group' is not a family dominated by the father; it is a maternal brood in which the male is usually not even present.* The segregation of the sexes is far more pronounced than their fleeting unions for sexual intercourse, which occur only in the mating season. Females represent the core of the primate group.[16]

If the male primate role in reproduction is necessary but minimal, if his sexual relationship with the primate female is ephemeral, and if his role in feeding and caring for infants is almost nonexistent, then how would the human male be feeling about his importance in life as he evolved out of the world of the primate male?

It seems to me very understandable that such males would want to create cultures that would say to them as men, "Look, you men are terrific!—even though you cannot do what the women do." *Perhaps because of these patterns from primate life, the personal freedom was available to males to create a more public life beyond the mother-child groupings—and they did. What men did everywhere was to set about creating for themselves "a culture to reassure"—patriarchy!*

Margaret Mead reports that "In every known human society, the male's need for achievement can be recognized. Men may cook, or weave or dress dolls or hunt hummingbirds, but if such activities are appropriate occupations of men, then the whole society, men and women alike, votes them as important. When the same occupations are performed by women, they are regarded as less important. *In a great number of human societies men's sureness of their sex role is tied up with their right, or ability, to practice some activity that women are not allowed to practice.* Their maleness, in fact, has to be underwritten by preventing women from entering some field or performing some feat.... There seems no evidence that it is necessary for men to surpass women in any specific way, but rather that *men do need to find reassurance in achievement, and because of this connection, cultures frequently phrase achievement as something that women do not or cannot do,* rather than directly as something which men do well."[17]

The power of technology
is the power to create.

Creating the solid propellant
that helps lift science
beyond the earth
is one way
we're using ours.

UNITED TECHNOLOGIES.

Pratt & Whitney Aircraft Group • Otis Group
Essex Group • Sikorsky Aircraft • Hamilton
Standard • Power Systems Division
Norden • Chemical Systems Division
United Technologies Research Center
United Technologies Corporation,
Hartford, Conn. 06101

2.

The Social Construction of Reality

Peter Berger and Thomas Luckmann in *The Social Construction of Reality*[1] provide a detailed explication of how this process of constructing a taken-for-granted social reality works. Berger and Luckmann are clear that our language is crucially important in this process, because our language daily builds images, shapes thought, and provides the boundary of what is thinkable as well as unthinkable. The Eskimos, for example, have more than forty words for snow. So many ways to describe snow enables the Eskimo culture to perceive nuances in the natural phenomenon of snow which are hidden from the rest of us.

Reality Is "Read In"

The point is that reality does not just exist "out there." Rather, we perceive reality through the eyeglasses of our social formulations. Do you remember the story of the Wizard of Oz? Dorothy and her friends were given green-colored eyeglasses when they entered the City of Oz, so that everything appeared green to them. A social construction of reality is like that. Let me give you several examples.

"HOW DO WE KNOW WE'RE NOT INSIDE SOMEONE'S PAPERWEIGHT?"

During the Spanish-American War an American gunboat approaching the remote Pacific Island of Guam fired a series of salvos at the Spanish fort guarding the island's main harbor. The Spanish governor of the island, not having received word of the war, had himself rowed out to the American gunboat to apologize for not having any gunpowder with which to return what he had interpreted as a twenty-one gun salute!

Now you would think that the firing of a cannon against a fort was a fact, an indisputable fact. But clearly the firing of the gunboat's cannon meant quite a different thing to that ship's captain, for whom it was a warlike act, than it meant to the island's Spanish governor, for whom it seemed a peacetime ceremonial gesture. Everything that happens to us we filter through the lens or screen of our understanding of our world.

Thomas Kuhn in *The Structure of Scientific Revolutions*[2] explores a specific instance of this process—the scientific community creating and amending its working paradigms or mental models of the world. It happens that in the decades preceding Galileo and Copernicus there had been a period of great interest in accurately observing the heavens. But suddenly the planet Uranus was discovered *after* it came to be widely accepted that the sun (and not the earth) was what the planets were orbiting around. Why had it not been discovered in that earlier period of great interest and accuracy in observing the heavens? No one was *expecting* planets to be orbiting the sun and no one was prepared to "see" what was unexpected.[3]

I understand from people who have done much more than I have with how the eye and the brain function, that even what we feel we observe is but a selection from the full multitude of sensory data with which we are confronted. Much of it, apparently, we simply don't take in. What we do perceive is determined by what our organizing paradigm or mental model is prepared to make sense of. The rest we dismiss as transitory phenomena, meaningless "noise."

Money, Cats, and Subatomic Physics

Consider the value we attribute to money. Our coins are really not worth very much in themselves. Our paper dollar-bills and our checks are absolutely worthless—except that we have all agreed to invest them with agreed-upon value. Together we construct that value, and then we all agree upon it and act upon it. Nowadays we don't even need paper money and paper checks; we have plastic cards and numbers and patterns in the electron streams in our computers, and we just manipulate the numbers and the flows of electrons. And everyone agrees these numbers measure value, and wealth.

"Thank you, sir, but I'd rather have money."

My husband and I share our living-space with a very interesting cat-personality. We have often pondered what our cat thinks of the way we spend our days. When she looks at us she sees two large and powerful human beings who do nothing but rearrange the paper in their lives. We get up in the morning and we look at paper. We type on paper by the hour. We receive paper from the mailcarrier. We take paper out to the mailcarrier. We are totally obsessed with paper.

Our cat must think our obsession with paper very odd. But it must be obvious to her that our obsession with paper and the markings it comes with and the markings we in turn make upon paper constitute a vast social construction of reality that we share with other human beings like ourselves, but to which she as our cat is not a party.

Or consider our dining room table. Ordinarily I say to myself, "I am a human and this table is wood. I have all these extraordinary potentials in myself, things I can do; I am animate and this table is inanimate. I am alive and this table is not." But a few years ago Fritjof Capra through his book *The Tao of Physics*[4] helped me get a layperson's grasp of subatomic physics. What I discovered was that at the basis of subatomic reality is what Capra describes as "probability patterns of energy"—which are the same for my dining room table as for me! Now once again, that is quite a blow to my everyday sense of things—or what I am calling here our social construction of reality.

Everything Is Standpoint-Dependent

Early in this century physicists doing the early research on subatomic reality discovered a very disturbing thing. They discovered that light for some purposes was a probability wave, but if you went at it in another way light appeared to be made up of particles. This vastly oversimplifies it, but as scientists first worked on this and were deeply puzzled, they came to realize that we can never know objective reality and there is no such thing as objective (or detached) knowledge. Everything we know is subtly influenced in the knowing by the standing point of the viewer. In a fascinating way these insights from subatomic physics and the sociology of knowledge have converged to underscore the subjectivity of *all* knowledge.

Drawing by Dana Fradon; © 1976 *The New Yorker Magazine, Inc.*

A philosopher summed this up for me recently in describing the major point of his most recent book: "Reason is standpoint-dependent."[5] That's it in a nutshell. Reason, scientific objectivity, everything, is standpoint-dependent. And we have usually not recognized this in the past. Everett Mendelsohn, currently chair of the History of Science Department at Harvard, tells of asking a group of MIT scientists to imagine a science that was not dominated by maleness, by elitism, by the profit-orientation, and by its relationship to war. This interested me because Mendelsohn could imagine a different science—but they could not. He could step out of current science and realize that the science we have created has been deeply colored by the profit system, the war system, the male system, and the elite system.

PLEASE KEEP
WITHIN THE
PARAMETERS

3.

Patriarchy as
a Social Construction of Reality

Berger and Luckmann assume—without acknowledging or examining their assumption—that it is male experience that has dominated this process of social construction. They are quite right in this, for our taken-for-granted social construction of reality has come to us through the eyes and ears, hearts and minds, images and perceptions—in short, the life experience—of the male. Our reality is standpoint-dependent, and it is the standing point of the male.

DDGray

Men have named and defined reality from their point of view, their standing point in the experience of life. The biblical account of Adam "naming" the world and everything in it (Gen. 2:19–20a) is a mythological account of a profoundly important truth in the sociology of our contemporary knowledge.

We live in Adam's world, for men socially constructed the reality which has defined and controlled how people would perceive their world.

"Little girls grow up and have careers because that's what little girls do."

Drawing by H. Martin; © 1980 *Punch*/Rothco.

If you doubt it has all been "named" from a man's experience, ask yourself why a computer, when it's working, is "up" and, when it's not working, it's "down."

But you may be asking—Why's all this a problem?—Why is culture being defined from the male standing point a conceptual trap for the whole human race?—Why is "Adam's world" a cul-de-sac not only for women but for the future of the human species?

The Male as the Human Norm

Patriarchy has a view of the human as normatively male: the illusion that when you've seen life from a male point of view you have seen life from the human point of view. We can see this aspect of patriarchy in every academic discipline. We have a male theology, a male philosophy, a male science, a male psychology.

It is not simply that males have been doing it. It is that until very recently the assumption has been universally accepted that what males perceive from the male point of view—philosophically, theologically, any way you want to talk about it—simply was the way the whole of humanity looked at that situation. What's truly extraordinary is to look back at certain things that happened really only yesterday, and to find that all sorts of theories were created using only males as the data base.

"Gentlemen, let us pool our expertise."

Moral Development through Male-colored Glasses

Lawrence Kohlberg at Harvard, for example, did some very important and fundamental work in moral development[1] in the late 1960s, work which everyone in the religious community heard about. Kohlberg developed a whole new understanding of what he called "the stages of moral development." He had given subjects hypothetical situations involving difficult moral questions, and he then categorized how his subjects made moral judgments. Kohlberg came out with a sequence of six stages, ranging from very inadequate moral thinking to very highly developed and principled moral thinking.

When I heard Kohlberg's work discussed in the religious community, nowhere did anyone say that the only research subjects Kohlberg had used were males. Yet Kohlberg and his stages were taken as the definitive word about moral development—by which was meant *human* moral development.

Carol Gilligan was a younger colleague teaching with Kohlberg at Harvard, and she wanted to base her research not upon Kohlberg's hypothetical moral situations but upon how people reasoned about real-life situations. She intended to interview young men making the decision about draft-resistance. But the Vietnam War ended, and by chance she chose the decision about abortion as an alternative real-life moral decision. Quite by accident Gilligan got an all-female data base. It turned out also to be very much of a socio-cultural cross-section because women of all sorts seek out abortion clinics.

What Gilligan discovered[2] was that women do moral reasoning very differently, and Kohlberg's stages simply did not fit what she was hearing from these women about how they were making this great moral judgment for their own lives. When Kohlberg had tried to put women into his stages, the women had rarely gotten past stage 3,

AN
AUTHORITY
FIGURE

because stage 3 is the last relational stage and stages 4 and 5 and 6 involve increasingly abstract moral rules and principles. As Freud had done earlier, some interpreted this as proof once again that women are morally deficient (because they do not do moral reasoning the way men do it).

In a Different Voice

Gilligan, on discovering what all these women were saying, recalled having heard something similar once before. Several years earlier she and Kohlberg had been teaching an undergraduate course together at Harvard, and twenty people had dropped out. Gilligan had been interested in why, and had gone to the trouble of extensive in-depth interviews with the drop-outs. Sixteen of the twenty turned out to be women. Gilligan described the reactions of these Harvard women later in her book, *In a Different Voice*—"Their thinking about moral decisions diverged from Kohlberg's orientation to individual rights, counterposing an ethic of responsibility and care to his concept of justice and fairness."[3]

Gilligan noted down their reactions, but because she had no mental categories to organize this data, she closed it up in a file folder in her drawer. She literally did not know what to do with that material. But later when she did the abortion work, she got out the data on the Harvard women and, yes, both sets of women were saying the same sort of things and were doing moral reasoning in a highly relational way. What they were saying did not involve the use of Kohlberg's abstract moral principles. Gilligan's women were saying, "I'm concerned about all these relationships in which I find myself—and I don't want to hurt anyone."

From MIT IAP catalogue.

It seems incredible to me that four years after Gilligan had first published her research in the *Harvard Educational Review,* Kohlberg in 1981 published *The Philosophy of Moral Development,*[4] and the book jacket trumpets his formulation of *"Six Universal Stages."* In Kohlberg's book Gilligan's work is treated in one paragraph and dismissed as a possible alternative variation on stage 6. The gender implications of her work are never acknowledged, and the limitation they imply for the "universal stages" is never even raised!

How long will male scholars in patriarchy go on with their delusion that being human and being male are synonymous? These male scholars live in a present-day intellectual milieu that supposedly understands the relativity (the standpoint-dependence) of all knowledge. How then can they go on refusing to acknowledge the relativity of their own gender standing point? How long can they ignore the sociology of their own knowledge?

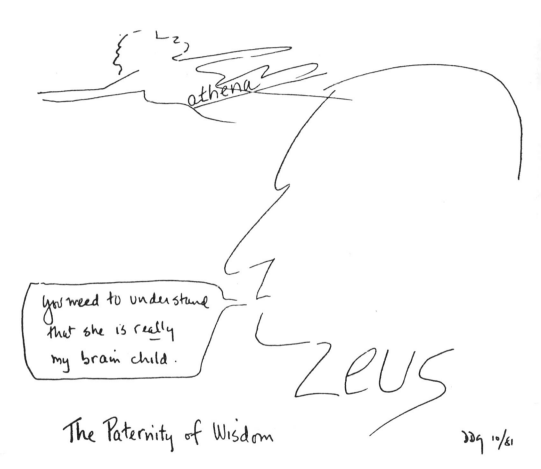

The Paternity of Wisdom

DDG 10/81

Drawing by Jerry Marcus; © 1981 *Good Housekeeping Magazine.*

"The difference between boys and girls is that we have zippers."

La Difference Is Non-stereotypic

Women today in all sorts of ways are beginning to say that, "Look, there are some interesting and absolutely non-stereotypical differences between male and female." They have nothing to do with the old theories in which the male is active and the female passive, or the male is intellectual and the female emotional. This has been hard for women researchers to put a handle on, but it has something to do with women feeling connected while men feel individuated, separate. Women's moral reasoning, for example, is an expression of a self that feels deeply embedded in relationships.

The work of sociologist Nancy Chodorow provides a helpful counterpoint to psychologist Carol Gilligan. In Chodorow's *The Reproduction of Mothering*[5] she writes about the psychodynamics of early childhood and points out that the male and female go through significantly different experiences in relating to the major nurturing figure within patriarchy—which is almost always female. As infants most of us have a very important experience of primary bonding to the nurturing person, usually mother. In the period between infancy and childhood the male-child discovers that mother is not the right sex to continue modeling himself on.

This creates a great problem for the male-child. If the father is not there very much (as is most often the case in modern industrial society), then the male-child cannot become male by establishing a personal identification with his father and embedding at first hand what it means to be a male. The girl-child sees mother and thinks, "Terrific, you're like me. I can model myself after you."

According to Chodorow the male-child whose father is much absent does not make this sort of close personal identification. Instead he makes what she calls a "positional identification" not with his father but with the male role. The boy-child does this by pulling away from that earlier selfhood which had been so invested with the mother. This means pulling away from all those very early warm and tender emotional and physical experiences of mother-child closeness. It often means pulling away from the warm and tender feelings in the boy-child himself (what Jungians mistakenly call his "feminine" self). He seeks instead to become male by becoming "not-female." So he distances himself from his mother. He distances himself from everything in his culture that is female. And he places himself very solidly in awe of all the things that are considered male in the culture.[6]

A Pulled-away Selfhood

Now all this is very interesting because, taken together with Gilligan, it explains why the male psyche develops as "self-in-separation" and the female personality develops as "self-in-connection" or "self-in-relationship." The daughter can keep growing while staying connected and still deeply and personally interrelated with the mother. The girl-child does not have to reject any of that process. Gilligan in her writing goes on to critique how male psychology—from Freud and Jung through Erickson and Kohlberg—has always imaged the self as growing and individuating *through separation*.[7] The male has always said it's important to be autonomous, to be individuated. You grow up by separating yourself from your parents.

Male psychology, Gilligan points out, has really been an extended explication of the inner life of the very autonomous, individuated, separated self.

This analysis does not lead to the conclusion that men are devils and women are angels. That is neither said nor intended.

The point is that everyone's consciousness bears the indelible marks of biology and life experience. Male consciousness has many strengths. It is also limited by the biological experiences and socialization of growing up male.

For reasons some of us are still trying to figure out, women don't seem to be put together that way psychically. Some of the new work in brain research, for example, indicates that women apparently also use the different hemispheres of their brains differently.[8] Women seem to have more of *both* hemispheres available to them, and at the same time, than men do.

Women's perceptions are also more contextual. In one experiment women of all ages were asked to fill in what the water level would be in a glass that is tilted. Men of whatever age respond the same way. A woman researcher tells of her eight-year-old son, who was asked to do this. He said,"Mother, this is so dumb, everybody knows the water level is parallel to the floor." And she said, "Wait until you see what your 15-year-old sister does with that." And he said, "Oh, come on, she's dumb but she's really not that dumb." His 15-year-old sister came in and drew the water level parallel to the top of the glass.[9]

There is evidence also of how much more women learn from their social context. When women and men are taken into a room full of people for 15 or 20 minutes and are then let out of the room, the women can answer very detailed questions about the context or environment of that room. Men simply do not pick up that sort of information.[10] Researchers are concluding that women, for whatever reasons, have greater contextual awareness— and that is why we as women do not draw the water level horizontal. The tilt of the glass influences us, the context influences us as women.

What the Other Eye Sees

Perhaps it is not surprising that the context influences us so strongly as women. The domestic world constitutes much of women's experience, and this experience teaches women to be intimately concerned not only about their own well-being but the well-being of the systems of which they are a part.

By contrast, the organizations men have made and managed so successfully in the larger world beyond the home have often focused on maximizing some part or factor, "suboptimizing" for efficiency, power, profit, or market share, for example.

In suboptimizing for one factor while ignoring the larger system, the complex and resilient social or environmental fabric can be stretched until it is distorted or even torn. In this way much that has been accomplished by suboptimization can be destroyed.

In dealing with her family, a woman has learned that she lives in a dynamic and complex system of interacting people, each with his or her own needs, goals, dignity, and feelings. Her family is a constantly changing system: the children grow up; experiences mature and age adults; accidents, illnesses, and death intrude from time to time. Operating within such systems, women know intuitively that you cannot consistently rob Peter to pay Paul, and that it is best to find ways to optimize the health, happiness, and long-term well-being of everyone within the system.

Dealing with Feelings

Strength and rationality, control and mastery, linear thinking and quantification—these are the traditional currency of the male world of thought and action. The traditional domain of the woman has involved living with weakness and emotion, vulnerability and helplessness, responsiveness and attention to the needs of others—in short, nurturing and caring for the world of children, the aged, and the home.

Thus, many of the more elusive and intangible aspects of our human life together have been delegated—or relegated—to women.

What are we to do when projects based upon traditional quantification and rationality will not work because factors seen to be "soft," uncertain, and unmeasurable (and therefore regarded as unimportant) in fact have proved to be very important?:

• What are we to do when "mastering the earth" is finally perceived to be causing our own destruction—since we ourselves are part of that earth and need it to sustain life?

• What are we to do when it appears we must do less mastering and controlling—and become more sensitive to what often seems "soft," unquantifiable, and emotional?

• How do we go about becoming more responsive and caring about our total situation, more attentive to consequences of our human activities, more nurturing of the world's total life-system?

Will men still strive to "rule" such a world by their old strategies? Will men place their hope in evolution and in time for the males of the species to become more responsive, more attentive, more nurturing?

Or will they find in themselves the humility—as well as the survival instinct—to draw upon the other half of human experience and allow women to give leadership and use the nurturing skills that life as a woman has taught them?

Women as tenders of the emotional fabric of life in the home have learned with practice ways of dealing with realities that are soft and elusive, real though intangible. Can we let women bring those skills into the male world? Or must men do it all themselves? Are men able to do it all themselves?

Living with Transitions

The transitional years ahead will involve shifts in perspectives, organizational structures, and in the mental models or paradigms we use to understand and organize our thoughts and experiences. It will be a time of heightened uncertainty for all of us.

To such a time women bring unique experiences and unique potential, for in their own life-cycle women have experienced—and are experiencing—similarly comprehensive transformations of their own identities and circumstances.

Consider the psychic flexibility demanded by the traditional American woman's life. As an adolescent she formed her identity as a single, independent individual.

Then, if she married (and she almost always did), she adjusted to living with another person in a society that expected her to take his name and to focus her identity and life around him and around the task of maintaining his home. She was uprooted and moved whenever and wherever it suited his career needs.

As her children were born, she became the hub of an expanding family. Each successive child became a spoke dependent on her centering care. It was the woman's lot to sustain and balance the family's life amid the diverse needs and activities of everyone in the family system. Men, of course, had families, too. But in the traditional marriage, men were not expected to focus their identities or adult lives upon their families but upon their work, their "careers." Men had careers; women had marriages and children.

Then slowly but with the inexorability of the calendar, the children grew up and left home. The woman's identity as mother faded in prominence. Her outlets for nurturing diminished within the family. In midlife she had to find a new identity and purpose for living to replace that of mothering.

She soon was back to life in a twosome, and she lived with the expectation that her husband would die before she did. She would then have to shape yet another identity as a widow, alone.

The traditional woman's life has been one of constant change. Just as she figured out how to balance life with two adults and one child, she had two children. Just as she had finally learned how to "safeguard without discouraging" an exploring toddler, she was confronted with a "terrible two" whose only word seemed to be "No!" She had no sooner figured out how to detour around the turbulent emotions of a two-and-a-half-year-old than her child was an angelic three whose major problem was one of diffidence.

Yesterday's strategies, born of last month's desperation, became quickly irrelevant to today's child and growing psyche. She constantly was devising new strategies to keep herself upright on the tightrope that was her life.

In this domestic life of the traditional American woman, there was always uncertainty. Nothing was sure. Nothing was quantified. All was elusive, emotional, responsive, intuitive. She was constantly monitoring her entire system for small feedback "signals" so that her behavior could adapt to changed needs.

She developed a tolerance for ambiguity, for moving through and riding with the waves and turbulence in her life. Those had a difficult time who were perfectionists or control-oriented in their personalities; adaptability and flexibility became the modes for successful coping and living.

The transition under way in global society involves heightened uncertainty for all of us. Living and coping most effectively with the uncertainties of this societal transition requires that leaders and organizations acknowledge their own lack of sureness about what they are doing and their own sense of vulnerability in these circumstances.

Insofar as acknowledging uncertainty and vulnerability is beyond the masculine mystique, our society will need to turn to women in this transition. Women can acknowledge their vulnerability and their lack of certainty without feeling their identity and femininity are threatened. Women are already accustomed to riding the uncertain waves of family life and—if we will allow them to—can help us in the "white-water living" of our future.

Biologically Programmed toward the Longer Term

The daily involvement of women with their children teaches them to look to the future. The chores that go with tending a two-year-old are not just for today. They are done in anticipation of the adult that child will grow up to be. Women's experiences of caring for their children inevitably expand their time horizons to include the world of their children's future.

This long-term orientation is badly needed in our present culture, in which the value of the future is often discounted. A dollar of expense (or income) a generation hence becomes almost invisible, as though hidden by a foreshortened time horizon.

How could men ever create an economic system that does this to the future? It cannot be accidental. It must be somehow related to the fact that in the world of men the next generation of children has never been at the center of men's attention, efforts, and hours.

What is there in the reproductive experience of the male that might cause him to feel involved in future generations? The male's one function of providing semen is overwhelmed by the sensation of orgasm, a sexual satisfaction he seeks innumerable times, in many contexts, and often with little reference to human reproduction.

Women, by contrast, experience nine intimate months of each child's gestation and then intense labor during birth. All this is often followed by long months of being on call for breast feeding the child. Don't ask that woman to accept a world view that ignores the life of the next generation!

There is still another subtle form of biological programming toward the long-term future that women have in common. Women during puberty become aware of the potential long-term consequences of their sexual encounters. In every sexual situation, they must balance the short-term pleasure of making love with the potential long-term costs of bearing and rearing a child.

If women do not immediately understand the long-term parameters of every sexual meeting, they alone pay the price for their lack of comprehension. Even in our day of ready access to means of birth control, it is usually the woman who must take the responsibility of making sure that some form of contraception is used. If she does not, the most extreme consequences—whether birth or an abortion—affect her body alone. Men are biologically able to walk away from the consequences of every sexual encounter.

No biological imperative conditions men to be sensitive to long-term consequences. But women's consciousness—which is so beautifully, albeit painfully, programmed to consider the longer term—has rarely been allowed into the boardrooms where decisions are made on corporate or public policy.

Yet our survival as a culture and perhaps as a species may depend upon our ability to adapt our dangerously foreshortened time horizons to longer ones with greater survival value. Policy made while devaluing the future is policy made with the female eye closed and with the female voice stilled, or ignored.

Gender as Analytic Tool

In addition to work being done about honest-to-god differences between males and females, true to who we are and not just the old stereotypes, there is also work being done by women scholars in which gender is being used as an analytic tool, much as race and economic class have been used as analytic tools.

In theology, for example, Judith Plaskow in *Sex, Sin and Grace* [11] shows how the male gender of theologians Reinhold Niebuhr and Paul Tillich greatly influenced their concepts of sin and grace. Sheila Davaney in her 1981 Ph.D. dissertation at Harvard explored how the male-gender definition of power has affected the way the power of God has been conceptualized in the thinking of two major 20th century theologians, Karl Barth and Charles Hartshorne. [12]

Drawing by Opie; © 1976 The New Yorker Magazine, Inc.

"Why are they doing that?"

In short, the assumption is really being called into question that the view from the male standing point is the only human view of anything. This is the real conceptual problem with so-called male generic language. It serves to perpetuate the illusion that "male" is synonymous with "human." Such identification is a conceptual trap. If human identity is born a twin,[13] then in the inner logic of evolution a balance of the two human perceptions may indeed be necessary for survival.

"We did it! We did it! You had good day and I had a good day—both in the same day!"

Consider the taking of risks. It is obvious to me that men, for whatever reasons, are more emotionally able to take risks and are more attracted to risk-taking than most women. There have been studies of attitudes toward nuclear energy (as well as many other things) that show that women are more averse to risk-taking than men.[14] Hennig and Jardim in their study *The Managerial Woman* express the view that women in business simply must learn to take risks.[15]

Laura Nader, an anthropologist, was asked to do a study of people working in the energy field. The results were reported in *Physics Today*.[16] What she found provides some very interesting comments about the masculine/feminine dimensions of our thinking about energy. She reports that among the men she interviewed, high-risk technology is considered masculine. She even heard people in California saying conservation is considered feminine. This is part of what Margaret Mead was getting at when she told Amory Lovins that she feared middle-aged men would never be able to accept an energy path that Amory had labeled "soft."[17]

The Sacred Canopy

The view of the human as normatively male has been buttressed by the view of cosmic reality as male. Remember God-the-Father, "He"? Peter Berger has written showing how the social construction of reality in human society is mirrored in what he calls the "sacred canopy"—the way we think about cosmic or religious reality.[18] Religion acts to legitimate our human social arrangements by projecting them as our sacred and cosmic frame of reference.

Consider this citation from Supreme Court Justice Joseph Bradley, writing in 1873, in a decision upholding the right of Illinois to deny a license to practice law to the first woman applicant, Myra Bradwell—"*The paramount mission and destiny of women are to fulfill the noble and benign offices of wife and mother. This is the law of the Creator.*"[19] You can see from this example why feminist theologians look at God-the-Father as a sacred canopy, which uses the religious dominance of a Male-in-the-sky tacitly to legitimate the dominance of the male in the order of things on earth.

Since God does not have genitals, it seems to me obviously inappropriate to describe God as either male or female. I also have little sympathy for adding "She" to "He" or "Mother" to "Father" when describing God. Both uses are too anthropomorphic for me to take seriously as religious concepts. I think these are steps backward rather than forward.

Now all this so far has been about what we can call conceptual trap number one. If indeed we need to balance the perceptions of the male with the perceptions of the female (and they are often different), then it seems to me utterly wrong to have the illusion that you have gotten all of human perception when you just ask for the male perception. It is a massive conceptual trap, and we've been caught in it for centuries, unfortunately for all of us. Male generic language only continues, reinforces and multiplies this conceptual trap.

Last night I watched an absorbing television docu-drama of Eleanor Roosevelt's years as our U.S. representative to the United Nations. I watched as her compassionate response to the displaced persons and suffering children after World War 2 evoked in her an overwhelming compulsion to draft a human manifesto—which became the UN Declaration of Human Rights. I watched her struggle to get all fifty-three nations then in the United Nations finally to agree upon its wording, a task her male colleagues considered wellnigh impossible.

As I watched, I was filled with admiration for the spirit of this amazing woman who, in her later years, had the energy and determination to make such an overwhelming contribution to the birth of a one-world consciousness. But even more I was filled with another amazement. How was it that I—who with an almost-adult awareness had experienced those years and was also something of a student of history—had not known that the UN Declaration of Human Rights was conceived and made possible by this remarkable woman? How was it that the work of all the male heads of state at Yalta, and George Marshall's role in the Marshall Plan, and the Truman Doctrine were well known to me, but Eleanor Roosevelt's crucial role in the gestation and birth of the UN Declaration of Human Rights had remained invisible to me?

The answer is simple but sad. It is clear and becoming clearer as women historians do their research in women's studies that patriarchal history works hard to make history the story of men, or literally *his* story! Women's accomplishments are *erased,* and when, like the UN Declaration of Human Rights, the accomplishment itself cannot be erased, the woman's crucial role in giving it birth is simply *not remembered.*

As my eyes moistened with tears of admiration for Eleanor Roosevelt's incredible accomplishment in caring enough to imagine the human manifesto, and then her incredible political and human accomplishment in bringing it into being against insuperable odds, I wept inside for all the other covenants of blessing which millions of other women might have brought into human history, had they ever been allowed to step onto the stage. What blessings to the human race have remained stillborn in the womb of history, because patriarchy insists that "all the world's a stage," and only men are allowed as actors upon it?

If the human species is indeed born a twin, can it possibly be in the self-interest of the species to allow so many possible scenarios of human benefit to remain unconceived and unborn in the womb of history? It is clear the male need to be (or illusion of being) the entire species has become dysfunctional and tragic for all of us.

4.

Imaging Our Place as Humans on Planet Earth

But even more important, I think, is the imaging of the place of the human self on planet Earth which has arisen from the male patriarchal system. This really has to do with what Walter Lippmann called "the pictures in our minds of the world beyond our reach."[1]

Myth #1 — Reality Is Hierarchical

Our first mental picture of ourselves on planet Earth comes from our Judeo-Christian heritage. You find it expressed most succinctly in Psalm 8, which says: "What is man that thou art mindful of him? Thou hast created him a little lower than the angels and have put everything else underneath his feet." And there you have the basic flaw in this mental picture, namely, a cosmic hierarchical ranking of values. The illusion is that you can look at reality, find out what the value of each thing is, and then rank it according to that which is more valuable (and is always "up") and has dominion over that which is of lower value (and is "down").[2]

The following visual summary of these relationships was developed for the Education Development Center in Newton, Massachusetts, for use in a school curriculum. It portrays the hierarchical nature of reality as imagined in our Old Testament heritage.

But I think this pyramid is also a true representation of many of the operating assumptions in our culture and in our own heads today. God is always visualized as "above." (Think of the hymns about "Spirit of God, *descend* upon my heart." God somehow is thought of as "up" and invisible, spirit.) Men clearly are above women. (St. Paul in the New Testament was clear that wives should obey their husbands, and St. Thomas Aquinas in the 13th century wrote that women were "misbegotten males.") Adults are above children in this hierarchy. (Children are supposed to obey adults, and in our legal system children have no independent "standing" but are either wards of the state or belong—are "owned"—by their parents, just as men used to own women.)

As I look back upon the biblical account of Abraham's near-sacrifice of his beloved son Isaac (Gen. 22:1–18), I now realize that the most remarkable part of the story is that if God had *not* stopped Abraham from killing his son as a blood-sacrifice to God, Abraham would never have been accused of murder or child abuse! In ancient Israel children, along with wives, concubines, slaves, and animals, were all the property of the male, to do with whatever he chose.

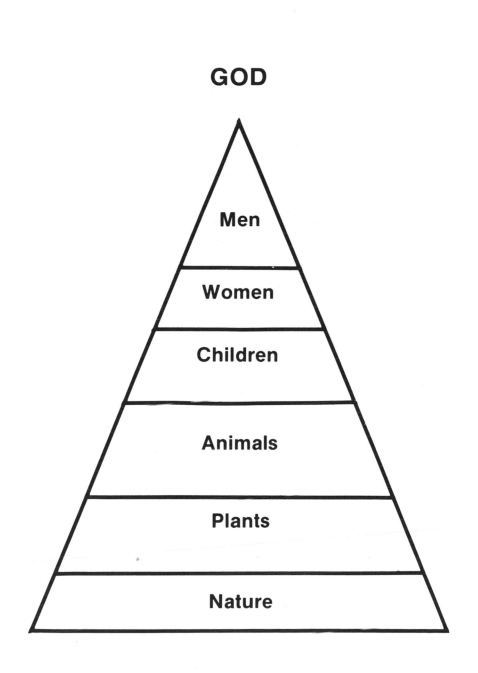

"BECAUSE YOU'RE A DOG... THAT'S WHY YOU CAN'T EAT AT THE TABLE WITH THE REST OF US!"

Humans are above animals in this view of things, and we clearly label them as subhuman. Plants are below animals, because they don't even have the grace to move around as we and the animals do but are rooted in the soil. And nature in this view is below everything else, completely material with no redeeming signs of spirit at all, consisting of inert rocks, stones, "dirt," and what we view as the "inanimate" world.

The assumption is that those which are below will obey those which are above. God is "above" in this mental picture from the Bible—and pure "spirit." "He" has put the human created in "His" image in place at the top of the ladder of being, and everything else is underneath "his" feet. And the illusion is that nature—which is always thought of and mythed as below—will accommodate.

Paul Santmire, author of *Brother Earth*[3] and a theologian who has studied the place of nature in Christian thought, has told me that often in Christian history the earth and nature have been visualized as simply the setting or stage upon which the cosmic drama of salvation between man and God takes place. Therefore nature has been a theological "non-category." It is like the floor or the ceiling—unimportant and, so-to-speak, a mere furnishing.

This picture of reality as a great ranked ladder of being, with "up" having more value than "down," is a very basic mental picture for us. It is so basic that it is simply assumed.

"That happens to be the Master's favorite chair, and I, not you, am the Master."

Myth #2—Man Is above Nature in Dominion

Mental picture number two is the evolutionary picture. That's interesting because when Charles Darwin wrote *The Origin of Species* and later *The Descent of Man,*[4] he was very aware that to tell humans who were given dominion by God (Gen. 1:26) that they were, indeed, descended from apes, was going to seem like a come-down. We were not going to like it. And we didn't, you'll remember.[5]

It took Christians a long time to deal with Darwin and the evolutionary picture of our place in nature. But we did, and I found it fascinating that, a century after Darwin, J. Bronowski could entitle his TV series and book *The Ascent of Man.*[6] He could do this because the mental picture you and I have of evolution is still the biblical pyramid or hierarchy of being and value—with God now absent from the top. The beginning of everything comes now not from God as spirit creating everything from above. Instead it all starts out in the primeval soup, and species emerge and evolve *upward* from below. We visualize the complex species on top, and the simple species underneath. That complexity should be more valued than simplicity is an interesting assumption. And, of course, we again are on the top and most valued!

"Obviously the work of a highly evolved intelligent species."

Drawing by Schochet; © 1981 *Saturday Review.*

"They're apparently intelligent, but so far all I've been able to train them to do is to stick a fish in my mouth whenever I jump through a hoop."

Confusing Uniqueness with Superiority

What we have done, it seems to me, is to confuse human uniqueness with superiority. All species are unique, as any biologist will tell you. We *are* unique. We uniquely feel and do some things other species do not. But they, on the other hand, do unique things that we don't.

In our trying to convince ourselves that human uniqueness does mean superiority, we have set up criteria that are always the criteria we felt we could win. We never asked ourselves which species has the best eyesight, because we wouldn't win that one. We never said, "Which species has the best hearing?" because we wouldn't win that one. We never asked, "Which species has the best ability to move swiftly?" because we wouldn't win that one either.

We thought we had the biggest brains, so we said "Which species has the biggest brain?" That obviously must be the most highly evolved species, and that was us! Now it appears from research on cetaceans (dolphins, porpoises and whales) that they have just as highly developed a cerebral cortex as we do.[7] They have an extraordinarily developed society, and they have the ability to echolocate one another. Their acoustical sensing of one another makes immediately transparent not only their location but also their physical health as well as their psychic state of anxiety or well-being. We humans obviously cannot do that. Indeed, we've never asked whether what humans do is as incredible as what plants do in photosynthesis—the direct conversion of solar energy into food and energy for themselves and all other living creatures. I'm not sure we do anything that is as incredible as photosynthesis—so we have never asked that question!

What we've done is make tremendous assumptions about the other species. We have said that the crucial thing we humans do is use language. But research with chimpanzees and even dolphins now suggests that they too can use language—and the controversy rages on!

"Although humans make sounds with their mouths and occasionally look at each other, there is no solid evidence that they actually communicate among themselves."

In religious circles people say to me—"But we *must* be superior, because cats don't pray." And I regularly answer, "How do we know cats don't pray?" Once you begin to question our built-in assumptions about the superiority of humans as contrasted with nonhumans, you realize our arrogance is truly staggering. We have *assumed* we knew what goes on in the consciousness of other animals, and that it wasn't much.

Some people have said the reason we have conquered the world is not because of our big brain but because of our thumb. The reason the whales and dolphins don't *conquer* the world the way we do is because they do not have the thumbs with which to make and use tools, and therefore their society has evolved in very different ways.

I have discovered in lecturing about the thesis of my book *Green Paradise Lost* that when you ask most people why they are convinced we are superior to animals, they will say, "Because we can kill them more than they can kill us." Now that's interesting, because if force is our criterion for superiority, then indeed the Nazis would be the superior race they claimed to be, because they killed more than any of the rest of us.

**What a piece of work is man.
How noble and admirable.**

Drawing by Auth;
© 1976. *The Philadelphia Inquirer.*

Joseph's Dream

The result of all this is an incredible anthropocentric illusion about ourselves and our place as a species on planet Earth. This view of ourselves has been the basis of Western science and technology. The assumption in all of our technology is that whatever we dream up in our majestic wisdom, nature will adjust to because it is below us and we were given dominion.

"How little we really own, Tom, when you consider all there is to own."

Or that we are the most highly evolved species and there-fore it's all done for us, and somehow or other the whole world will always adjust to what the most highly evolved species decides to do.

"I mean, you can have the cleanest air in the world but if you can't manufacture anything what the hell good is it?"

Our dreams of dominion remind me of the Old Testament patriarch Joseph's dreams as a youth (Gen. 37:5–11). You'll perhaps recall how the teenager Joseph dreamt that his older brothers bowed down to him, and dreamt another time that even the sun and moon and stars bowed down to him. These were wonderfully uplifting dreams for Joseph and perhaps great for his ego. But unfortunately the dreams were not true to the reality of his circumstances, and his brothers resented being put down by their younger brother and proceeded to "do him in" (Gen. 37:23–36).

Similarly, when we ponder the immensity of a created universe filled, scientists now think, with 190 billion galaxies, ours have got to be delusions of grandeur on a large scale for us to think that we as one species on a speck in a tiny portion of one galaxy have been given dominion over it all!

The truth about life is that we exist in a self-managing universe. Our planet manages itself. We are actually like a fetus within a placenta, i.e., totally dependent upon biosphcral cycles for our existence in life.

Through the thin cell layer of the finest root threads of the placenta, carbon dioxide and waste products flow out of the blood circulation of the fetus, while oxygen and nourishment are taken in.

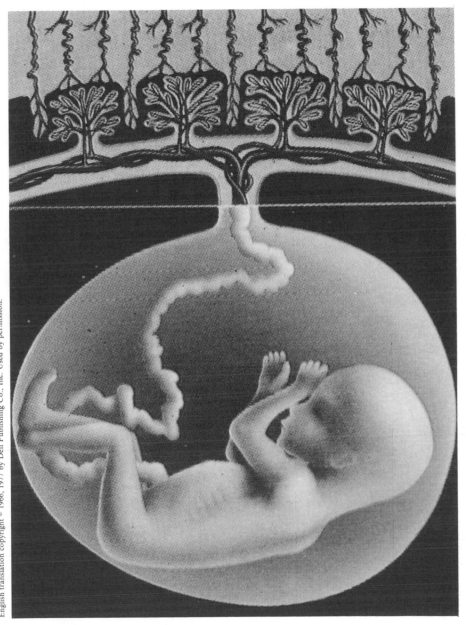

But we have the illusion that we somehow must manage the earth—because we think God has given us dominion over it. And even if we haven't done it right today, we're still convinced that tomorrow we'll do it perfectly! We seem able to go on thinking this way despite mounting evidence that we don't think wholistically enough to anticipate all the multiple unforeseen effects of everything we do.

"Now, this should clear up your psoriasis.
But the side effects may turn you into a frog."

Today that illusion of dominion is expressed as "stewardship." In my travels I keep telling the religious community—and they don't like it much—that the concept of stewardship is still totally paternalistic. It still assumes we know what we are doing, that we can indeed manage planet Earth. If I've learned anything these past few years, it is that we do not know yet what systems we disrupt by what we do in human interventions. Every day we are learning new things we have inadvertently done.[8]

Finishing the Copernican Revolution

What I'm talking about is finishing the Copernican Revolution. It's not accidental that humans began thinking that they were at the center of the universe and the sun and all the planets went around them. It felt really cozy for us to think that way. Except, of course, that astronomically it was simply untrue. With difficulty we have adjusted our thinking about the skies and solar system. But having gotten our astronomy straight, we left the rest of our mental pyramid of value and being in place in our heads. Once again, it feels great for us to say that we are at the top of everything.

"Why, no! Why should I ·feel small? I've just been put in charge of the whole Eastern region."

We must finish that Copernican Revolution in our heads, because hierarchical thinking not only ranks diversity but it also legitimates the oppression of people and of nature. It is not accidental that in order to do what they did to the Jews, the Nazis had to create an elaborate rationale that the Jews were subhuman. And they did. It is not accidental that in order to do to Blacks what we did in slavery, we again had to create a rationale (again using our Judeo-Christian heritage) that Blacks were sub-human. And at the time when we are eliminating other species, and possibly eliminating the whales, it is also not accidental that the movie *Jaws* comes out. One of the things mythology does is stand reality on its head, so that just when we are endangering whales as a species, we create a movie in which a large fish is after *us*. Very interesting!

Drawing by Ketchem; © 1973 Field Newspaper Syndicate.

"...AND THIS *GIANT CARROT* WAS CHASIN' ME AND SAYIN', '*EAT ME! EAT ME!*'."

This ranking of diversity has come from patriarchy. Males created a society in which males were ranked above females. From this, that male thought-world of patriarchy got into ranking all diversity. We have developed veritable contact lenses through which we now look every time we encounter diversity. And we always ask ourselves, "Which of us is better?" Whites look at Blacks and ask, "Which of us is better?" Civilized look at "primitive" and ask, "Which of us is better?" And educated look at uneducated and ask, "Which of us is better?" Whether we realize it or not, these are strange questions! Even in academia we hear, "My thinking is better than your thinking."

Diversity does not exist to be ranked. But in this patriarchal culture we simply do not know how to deal with diversity without ranking it. It does not occur to us simply to appreciate it or honor it.

"YOU'RE A CREEP!"

Drawing by Schochet;
© 1974 *Good Housekeeping Magazine*.

Myth #3—Nature Is Feminine

Now unfortunately for us there is a third mental picture. That is the picture you get any time nature overwhelms us. Whenever hurricanes, snowstorms, floods, or any big natural events overwhelm human society, some person in the press or TV is going to talk about how "Mother Nature" zaps us again.

I have often asked myself, "Why don't we heed our environmental warnings more?" It should be so plain to us. It is not that we are unintelligent, but why don't we pay more attention?

During a trip to Iceland several years ago I discovered an outdoor larger-than-life statue done by Iceland's major sculptor Asmundur Sveinsson. It was of a large bosomy woman bending nude over a toddler who is sitting up sucking on one breast while the mother-figure indulgently is kissing the child's head. The outdoor sculpture is not titled, but a small prototype in the artist's studio is labeled "Mother Earth."

David Dodson Gray after Sveinsson.

Checking Mother Earth's pulse for signs of new oil

Oil explorers say the easy oil's been found. For this Gardner-Denver seismograph rig, that goes double. It must penetrate a centuries-old layer of permafrost as well as rock before studies can begin. Wherever in the world important work is done, you find Gardner-Denver on the job. We're helping build better roads. Our equipment drills tunnels through mountains to bring water to power generating stations. In mining, Gardner-Denver is the name everyone knows and respects. And in manufacturing our air tools and hoists are helping increase productivity in industry after industry. See what we can do to help you. Gardner-Denver Company, Dallas, Texas 75247.

Gardner-Denver seismograph drilling rig at work on the North Slope. Photo Courtesy Imperial Oil Limited.

It has finally begun to dawn upon me that just below the conscious mind there is that powerful encompassing sense of "Mother Nature." And what will "Mother" do? Mother will always feed you and clothe you and carry away your wastes—and never kill you, no matter how nasty you are, because mothers don't kill you.

Dorothy Dinnerstein in *The Mermaid and the Minotaur*[9] writes of the origins of these feelings we have that nature and the environmental "surround" are somehow female. Woman is the primary nurturing figure of patriarchy. From the time we are babies we all experience the very earliest confusion between the "surround" and our mothers. As adults we still have difficulty believing our surroundings really are impersonal or, on the other hand, that our mothers are really fully human persons.

The advertisements you have just seen are typical; I clipped them from a selection of recent magazines. As this easy imagery of feminized nature suggests, most of us do not really understand (or feel) how impersonal the environment is. The fact is that natural systems out there will not weep one tear when humans can no longer breathe or function on planet Earth. They could not care less (or more). But somehow it makes us feel good to personalize those impersonal cycles into a sense of Mother Nature.

Contrarywise, we have difficulty understanding that our own mothers are real people. In a parallel vein, a study several years ago showed that most college students do not think their parents have sex; perhaps they did (at least once), but not any more. A mother is not allowed to be that much a fully human person!

Nature as Compliant Woman

There are some other interesting confusions going on too. There is nature-as-woman-with-power, of course, symbolized as "Mother Nature." But then there is also in our heads nature-as-compliant-woman, the woman who is below. In *Green Paradise Lost* I called this nature-as-patriarchal-wife and "mother-in-chains."[10]

You find this view of feminized nature in such phrases as "virgin resources" and "the rape of the earth." Male vocabulary here is almost a Rorschach test when you get into the words. "Virgin" resources are not "made love to" but "exploited." One evening I sat in the MIT Faculty Club and had a visiting scientist tell me seriously that the resources in the ground were, in his words, "crying out to be used." He was serious. And he didn't even realize what he was saying. In such a world I would hate to be a virgin resource, because I consider virgins an endangered species!

We have to come to terms with our illusions about feminized nature, because they serve to legitimate the exploitation of nature by a male-dominated culture. The feeling is widespread among us that what we find in nature is the basic compliance of a female waiting to be used by the culture, a culture which is always symbolized as masculine.

Potlatch

We're partners with Mother Nature. But we help her hurry the process.

Right now every person in the country uses about 575 pounds of paper products a year. Twenty-five years from now they'll probably require twice as much.

So when you're a tree farmer and wood converter like Potlatch, you have to hurry nature along a bit to meet the need.

She can use help. Where it takes her a century to grow a new crop of trees, we can add science to her good instincts and grow a new crop in 70 years. Soon, we expect it to be substantially less.

At Potlatch we have genetic programs to produce super trees in one part of the country. In another, we let nature do her job through natural seeding. We also help with selective thinning, planting, and controlled fertilization of our 1.3 million acres of prime forest lands.

This partnership between nature's sure instincts and Potlatch forestry science enables us to harvest several hundred million board feet of logs each year. We then convert this renewable resource into lumber, plywood, specialty wood products, particleboard, paperboard, business and printing papers, packaging and disposable consumer paper products.

Our partnership with nature helps us meet America's growing wood and paper need. But it's also good business. In 1974, Potlatch sales were $488 million—up from $442 million in 1973. Earnings in 1974 were $45,289,000, or $6.20 per share, a one-third increase over $33,979,000, or $4.85 per share in 1973, which more than doubled the $16,585,000, or $2.24 per share earned in 1972.

If you'd like more facts about Potlatch—an equal opportunity employer—just ask. Write: **Potlatch Corporation, P.O. Box 3591, San Francisco, CA 94119.**

Reprinted by permission of Potlatch Corporation.

In patriarchal society, culture is always perceived as masculine—"man" and "mankind." If you doubt that, let me tell you of a book I was reading several years ago which talked about the impairment of the intellectual life. The phrase chosen totally unselfconsciously was "the *castration* of the intellectual life." The intellectual life was sensed as fundamentally masculine. So if you're going to hurt the intellectual life, you castrate it. You don't rape it.

One day my husband and I were in a local rug shop picking up a small rug. The young man who brought the rug up from the basement threw it down on the floor and said, "There she is." My husband mused aloud, "Why is that rug a 'she'?" The young man looked totally astonished and said, "I don't know." And I said, "I do—because you put it on the floor and walk on it, and there's no way you're going to call it a 'he'!"

Once we begin to get into this, we realize that there seem to be interesting inner processes going on that delineate precisely for us which pronoun feels appropriate and which sort of imaging we find it congenial to use in terms of what is sensed to be feminine and what is sensed to be masculine.

If We Imaged Nature as a Pink Kangaroo

I am trying very hard to get those of us who are active in the environmental movement to take our feminizing of nature seriously. Male environmentalists do not want to deal with this aspect of our environmental problems. But I am convinced that if we imaged nature as a pink kangaroo, we would have blue-ribbon academic committees examining how we think about and treat pink kangaroos in our culture, because that would be seen as germane to the problem. But since we image nature as feminine—either as overpowering mother or as a compliant virgin to be used—we will not yet deal with this.

Yet we cannot in my opinion separate the rape of the earth from our culture in the United States where a woman is violently assaulted every eight seconds. These two cannot be separated. They must be dealt with together because they are profoundly interrelated. We also cannot separate the quaint way economics has always conceptualized the environment as "free goods" (which will always be there freely supplying your needs) from the way in which women have been dealt with in patriarchy. Women also have been considered "free goods," always there supplying your needs, whether as mother or as patriarchal wife. There is just no way to separate how we have dealt with these things.

"A-a-ah! Can't you just feel yourself unwinding?"

You can glimpse all of these issues in the Fischetti cartoon of the earth disintegrating like a rotting tomato. My husband and I used this cartoon for several years in our lecturing as a way of portraying what we are doing to the earth, for in truth we are "eating" our children's future. Or as someone else has said, "We'll eat the chicken today, and leave you the feathers for tomorrow." You can almost feel the chill of realization shiver over an audience confronted with this Fiscetti cartoon.

But look again at the cartoon, for it illustrates not only that we are consuming our children's future but also our "illusion of dominion." The father stands on top of the globe, assuming that it is *all his,* and he feels badly that he cannot pass on to his son the ownership of the planet.

But look still again at the cartoon, this time with a woman's eyes. Did it strike you as strange that the patriarchal father is passing the ownership of the planet on to his son—and the woman who gave birth to the son is not even in the picture? In the patriarchal illusion of "owning" the planet, women are simply not thought of and thus are truly "invisible."

"My boy, someday none of this will be yours!"

Drawing by Jerry Marcus; © Good Housekeeping Magazine.

"Someday, if you're not careful, all this will be yours!"

I conclude from all this that we have three myths running around in our heads and we must come to clarity about all of them. The first myth is that *reality is hierarchical,* i.e., that diversity can be ranked. The second is that *generic Man is above nature in dominion.* And the third myth is that *nature is feminine.* All of these are deceptive illusions. They are distortions of the reality of what is, and continuing to live by such distortions will kill us.

5.

The Trap of Separation

There Is No Future for Illusion

A conceptual trap is a trap because it doesn't fit the reality of what is. It was formulated when apparently you thought it fit reality but the reality has changed. Or perhaps it never did fit and you just didn't know it. In either case it must be changed because it is so much of an illusion that if we continue to function on the basis of it we will destroy ourselves on planet Earth.

I wrote in *Green Paradise Lost* that "Ultimately, the problem of patriarchy is conceptual. The problem which patriarchy poses for the human species is not simply that it oppresses women. Patriarchy has erroneously conceptualized and mythed 'Man's place' in the universe and thus—by the illusion of dominion that it legitimates—it endangers the entire planet."[1]

"Why aren't you all at work?"

My contention is that patriarchy has been obsessed with ranking diversity because it has been obsessed with ranking male and female. And we can't give up ranking diversity unless we give up ranking male and female. It is all tied together. Because we have lived with mental hierarchies of value, we have never been able to understand life systemically. Yet we are living in a system that is highly interrelated and therefore must be understood systemically if we are to survive. And the selves that have been formed by and identified with patriarchy have not been able to feel connected to that interrelated reality. That's what Chodorow is talking about—the psychodynamics by which the male develops a self that is more aware of being separated than of being connected. "With no need to repress or deny their earliest attachment, girls can define and experience themselves as part of and continuous with others. . . . boys must repress these same attachments as they shift their identification from mother to father. That means that they must distinguish and differentiate themselves in a way that girls need not. . . .they come to define and experience themselves as more separate from others; . . . adult masculine personality comes to be defined more in terms of denial of connection and relations."[2]

And that separated self then creates theology, philosophy, psychology—all of which spin out worldviews of separation of self from self, of Man from Nature and the world from God.

"*Who sets the tone here?*"

"But all I did was ask for a dime!"

Patriarchy as a Great Trap

A great trap is one that is at the root of many other traps. When I was in graduate school at Yale Divinity School I sat through discussions in philosophical theology that got so abstract I just could not bear it any more. I would simply do laundry lists or other things while the abstractionists finished their discussions. I have since discovered that this experience is common to many women. This kind of abstraction—in which the mind just hops around with its nimbleness in abstraction totally cut off from everyday reality—is something a great many women have little patience for.

I have had a similar experience with male psychologists and their too-ready acceptance of not the mind in its nimbleness but of the self-in-separation. I was reminded recently when reading Gilligan that a decade or so earlier I had been confronted with raising a then-teenage daughter, and I had found then that I simply could not accept what male psychologists were saying about how to deal with teenagers. They were saying that in order for teenagers to become autonomous selves, they literally had to blow their parents out of the water and break the parental tie quite traumatically. What we as parents were supposed to be was sufficiently authoritarian to make all this necessary in order for them to take control of their own lives. I thought the whole thing was unnecessary and dumb!

I convinced my nice husband that it was dumb. My thought was that you give a teenager control of his or her life because, indeed, you couldn't live their lives, and you didn't know what was going to be right for them. And then you said, "Look, you've got the control, your life is yours. We'll support you in whatever you decide." My feeling was (and is) that when they are teenagers, they need their connections with their parents even more than at almost any other time in their lives. Teenagers need *less* destruction rather than more in these vital relationships in order to become themselves, and if you aren't standing in the way of their decision-making and their taking responsibility for their own lives, then they don't have to blow you out of the water.

Until I read Gilligan and Chodorow I didn't know why I had had those gut feelings. I hadn't made the intellectual distinction between maturing *within* relationships (which is what women are expected to do and what women do indeed conceptualize themselves as doing) and the male way of *separating yourself from* relationships "in order to grow."

What I've been trying to indicate by these examples is that patriarchy is indeed what we might term a Great Conceptual Trap, because it seems to be at the root of so many other conceptual traps. But there is more, for out of patriarchy have come vast and inclusive—even cosmic— ways of viewing ourselves as isolated, separate, apart from one another, and to this we now turn.

119

Cosmic Tapestries of Separation

Several centuries of an unacknowledgedly male interpretation of the human situation reached a culmination in Ernest Becker's *The Denial of Death*.[3] The basic human predicament—according to Becker, according to 20th century neoorthodox Christian theology, and according to a nearly century-old tradition of existentialism and modern depth psychology—is one of anxiety. We are (in Becker's words) "gods with anuses."

That's so fascinating. Here the human is seen as intended by his spiritual dimensions and his capacities for self-transcendence to be a god. Yet still he is trapped in this dumb body that defecates, ages and dies. It is small wonder that such a person feels crucified between spirit and body—and is anxious. This is indeed a terrible predicament, and so different from the sense emerging among women that women view themselves very differently and feel connected to one another and to nature. Yet Becker won a Pulitzer Prize for his book, and in some circles it is considered a pinnacle of psychology and existentialism.

It is important for us to see here that the dualism of mind/body and spirit/flesh Becker so vividly describes are a logical consequence of the separation which patriarchy posits between the world of spirit (God) and the world of matter (Nature). In their philosophy and theology and psychology males have created what have become cosmic theologies of separation, rather than of connection. And to live by cosmic theories of separation when you are actually within an interconnected reality-system is dangerous to the health and well-being of human society.

*"That's your answer, sir? 'I got mine, the
hell with everything'?"*

"I'm sorry. My responsibility doesn't go beyond this bubble."

Male culture must accept responsibility for the fact that we have conceptualized ourselves as separated—and that all this is a product of the male psyche. It has indeed been "a man's world." And now men must accept responsibility for how they have thought about that world as well as for how they have lived in it.

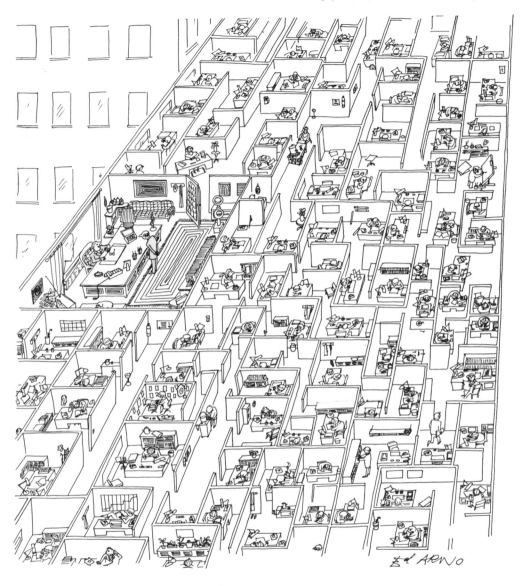

"I'm afraid a raise is out of the question, Benton,
but in view of your sixteen years of service
we are advancing you two spaces."

The Very Different Sense of Being Connected

We are not separated from one another. Nor are we apart from the air and water and energy which flow through and are vital to our bodies and our well-being. We are not separate from but participate in nature. In short, we are profoundly interconnected. The dawning systemic understandings in field after field are confirming the reality of our interconnection.

Drawing by MCD; © 1981 Saturday Review.

In a fascinating way women's spirituality, long denied by patriarchal religion, is confirming and conceptualizing that connectedness. Carol Christ in *Diving Deep and Surfacing*[4] (and earlier in a book she coedited, *Woman-Spirit Rising*[5]) tells us about many women having mystical experiences in relation to nature. In these experiences they do not consider nature to be God but they find the Ultimate to be profoundly present. Such experiences of Presence signify a profound connectedness to and resonance with the rest of the universe.

Carol Christ was doing her graduate study in theology at Yale in the early 1960s when she first began focusing upon women's spirituality and its distinctive nature mysticism. Nearly every male theologian there told her, "That's not religion—nature worship perhaps, but not religion." What we now know they were saying was, "That is not religion as we male theologians have developed it." It was not in the same room, it was not even in the same ballpark!

What is emerging now is that women have a very interesting and different religious consciousness which includes a strong sense of connectedness to the natural world. Thus women have a deep sense of "feeling at home" on planet Earth.

"Your wife's on the phone. The azaleas are out."

Under patriarchy we humans have been attempting to become as gods and transcend our mortality. We have mythed ourselves as "apart from" and "above." We have never made our peace with being rooted in flesh, mortals who could be at home on this planet.[6]

6.

Looking Ahead

Delegitimating the Divine Right of Humans

There is historical precedent for what we are undertaking, and it is useful to examine it. Western nation-states emerged from the medieval period with the institution of monarchy. The legitimacy or "rightness" of kings to their judicial and law-giving role was powerfully buttressed by what came to be known as "the divine right of kings." Just as it was unthinkable for a body to live and not have a head, so it was thought that the nation could not exist without its head, the monarch.[1] It was all seen as a part of God's plan that peoples and nations have divinely instituted authority ruling over them.

But in building up to the first of the modern revolutions, the Puritan Revolution in England under Cromwell in the 1600s, a people's and a nation's consciousness underwent a transformation. John Milton's epic poem *Paradise Lost* was in part a political and theological tract undermining the view that in God's plan there had to be kings over people, i.e., the divine right of kings.

Today we have a general consciousness that legitimates the divine right of the human species to "rule" the earth. Again, the myth is that the lion is "king of the beasts"; in fact, the human species claims that function. My book *Green Paradise Lost* can be viewed as a tract calling upon us to **de**legitimate that rule of the human species

If, as I have urged, we are in this Creation like fetuses within a placenta, then our role in relation to the planet is one of **attunement**—getting in tune with the (nonhierarchical and systemic) reality of life in our earth system, and then living our lives and civilization accordingly.

Setting the Balance Straight

What do I see for the future of male and female in this attunement? I want to assure you I do not wish to see matriarchy replace patriarchy. I do not feel that matriarchy would be any improvement upon patriarchy.

Throughout the past history of the human race as it has lived in a variety of patriarchal cultures, the unique perspective and potential of women has been ignored or disregarded. To continue to do this is to proceed into the future like a person born with two eyes, who insists upon wearing a blinder over one eye. Obviously such a person will never see in three dimensions, for that can only be done with two eyes open and working.

To change the metaphor, it is like a person born with two ears trying with only one audio channel to hear some recorded music reproduce the original three-dimensional sound—when two related but distinct and different audio signals are needed to recreate the original reality.

What I'm saying is that the human species has, so to speak, been driving down the highway of life with one eye (the female) held firmly closed. We have listened to the music of life with one ear completely blocked. Certainly this is strange behavior. For a two-gender human species interested in survival, it seems curiously maladaptive and self-destructive.

What we need to work toward is a balance in perceiving—so that we perceive reality with a stereo-scopic vision and incorporate into all that we do both the way males see reality and also the way females see reality. Our problem now is that our survival as a species on the earth is threatened by the spread of a monoculture—a scientific and industrial and militaristic culture created out of the male consciousness. After three or more thousand years of patriarchy we confront a huge and highly developed ballooning out of masculine consciousness. We also have another tiny consciousness, which has scarcely begun to emerge among the females of our species. As Elizabeth Janeway has said, women are "between myth and morning," just awakening into a truly "female" consciousness.

Drawing by Cary Grossman;
© 1980 *Saturday Review.*

I have observed that people get nervous very quickly when you talk too much about women. Even women will say, "Let's talk about humans." But I don't think you can balance men's consciousness and women's consciousness yet—because male consciousness is so dominant and authentic female consciousness is so tiny and awakening. If we desire genuinely to balance the human perception of reality, we must all—males and females—nurture the birth of authentic women's consciousness.

The Future of Wholistic Thinking

There is much talk among futurists about the need for wholistic thinking. But let's be clear that we'll never arrive at the Elysian fields of wholistic thinking so long as we continue to dwell in the thought-traps of patriarchy. One cannot think systemically or wholistically and still think in hierarchies. Systems analysts have understood a lot about the interrelationships within systems. Yet they still use the terminology of *higher* and *lower* systems. The unquestioned assumption seems to be that systems which are complex are "higher" than systems which are simpler. What could (and in my view, should) have been said is simply that some systems are components that nest within and interact with more inclusive systems. One misses the full richness of interaction in the life and behavior of such systems when one is intent upon imposing irrelevant and arbitrary value-structures (such as hierarchy) upon the behavior of complex biological or social systems.

130

Sure you're in line for a promotion.

But ironically one cannot stop imposing such arbitrary value-structures until one has perceived them, and until one has acknowledged how such imposed value-structures have functioned. Then one must trace them to their root in our highly subjective and personal needs to *rank* male and female. Finally we must comprehend our personal need to project upon the world these value-structures that make *us* feel good about ourselves. We must come to see that within patriarchy the ranking of diversity has been a pervasive and contagious disease. Thus as we try to move into a future of more wholistic thinking, it is crucial for us to come out of patriarchy.

Drawing by Saxon; used by permission of the artist.

Honoring Diversity

Coming out of patriarachy means first of all honoring diversity. To honor diversity is to respect the creation-based value of everything that is. To say that something is of value because it happens to be of use or value to humans simply does not reflect the complex reality of life. Every part of the system, every species, makes a distinctive contribution to the working of the entire system of life.

Drawing by Vadun; © 1981 *Saturday Review.*

"Of course I'm impressed by the way you unerringly made your way across 800 miles of trackless waste to be united with your master. Unfortunately, he moved last week without leaving a forwarding address."

Drawing by M. Twoby; © 1980 *Saturday Review.*

A system is a sustained pattern of behavior in which everything affects everything else. You can't rank the diversity that maintains a system because each element has its part to play. They all are important. Hence the value of each part of that system has its basis in creation. Each part is of radically equal value—because all are a part of and contribute to life in the system.

I might say, incidentally, this sends traditional theologians of the Judeo-Christian tradition "up the wall." If you think they have a problem with not ranking male over female, I want to tell you they really have problems with the notion that they are not of more value than the mosquito or the sparrow! But the ecological reality is that each species has its own unique function in the community of life.

Drawing by Donald Reilly; © 1981 *The New Yorker Magazine, Inc.*

Reality has always been a seamless web of interrelated systems. Within patriarchy we have simply tried to superimpose our humanly generated hierarchical paradigms onto that reality in much the same way that we projected in earlier times a pre-Copernican astronomy upon the skies. The result has been incredible anthropocentric illusion and our now fast-approaching ecological disasters. Repentance involves taking off our Wizard-of-Oz hierarchical glasses and allowing ourselves, for once, to perceive the systemic reality in which we actually live as earth-creatures.

There's nothing
quite like the warm
feeling you get inside
when you learn
you've just been
elected class tree.

Kodak film. For the
times of your life.

Reprinted courtesy of Eastman Kodak Company.

Coming Out of the Patriarchal Closet

Coming out of patriarchy, then, means: (1) coming out of ranking diversity and into honoring diversity within genuinely systemic thinking; (2) coming out of confusing the human with maleness and *vice versa,* so that we can have truly stereoscopic male/female perception; and (3) coming out of anxiety and self-as-separation to see the self-as-connections—perceiving the human situation not as one of managing the earth but as being one among many participants affecting and sustaining life on earth.

Patriarchy is a great and usually invisible conceptual trap. It is great because it is the root trap underlying so many other small conceptual traps. It is invisible because it is so pervasive we take it for granted. How unlucky we are that it is especially invisible to those men who dominate today's cultural systems!

Unless we come out of patriarchy, we will never "make it" in this system of planet Earth because patriarchy underlies too much of the thinking and "doing" which threaten ultimately not just women but the survival of our species. Like fish swimming in the sea of our own cultural assumptions, we must continue to ask: What additional assumptions are there which are rooted in our male/female relationships and thus work quite unconsciously in our collective minds to undergird (and perhaps even conceal) what we are doing to ourselves, our world and our future?[2]

Drawing by Mankoff; © 1980 *Saturday Review.*

MANKOFF

We must now re-myth our human situation. It is time for a new cosmic vision—a new understanding of human life in its setting on the earth. One way I have described our situation is to compare us to a group of four or five dancers, dancing round and round rapidly, holding one another's hands and leaning back. As we dance, in our movement all are holding one another in existence. This dancing circle is the circle of life we share with all the other species and the entire planet. It is "a symbiotic dance of cosmic energy and sensual beauty, throbbed by a rhythm that is greater than our own, which births us into being and decays us into dying, yet whose gifts of life are incredibly good, though mortal and fleeting."[3]

Elizabeth Gibson Ferry

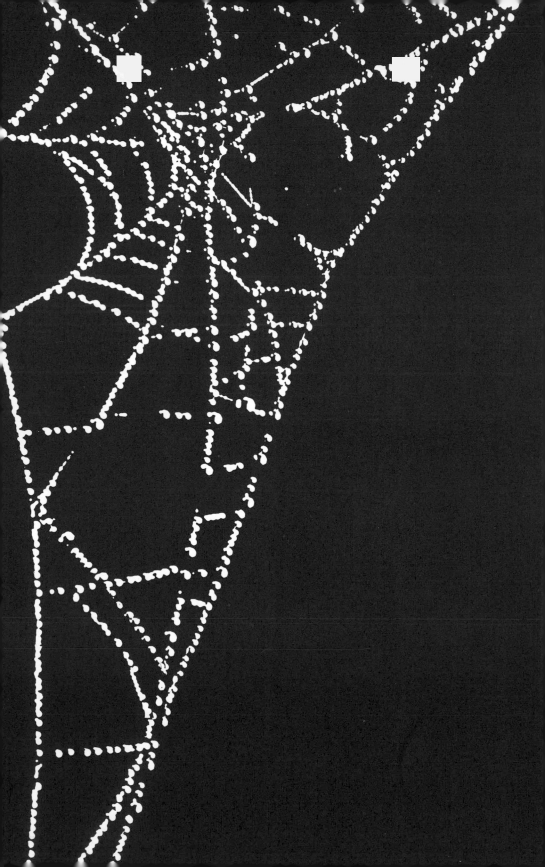

Notes

About Conceptual Traps

1. The term "conceptual trap" in the title was a creation of Wilson's, as we brainstormed together in connection with the USA/Club of Rome member meeting in April 1981 a more "popular" way of expressing the notion of a social construction of reality.
2. This note on conceptual traps is adapted from a memorandum prepared for the USA/Club of Rome membership meeting, April 14–15, 1981. At that meeting Thomas W. Wilson, Jr., discussed the urgency of a new concept of national security that is relevant to the 1980s and 1990s—for the conceptual trap of inherited geo-political doctrine threatens to lead to the only future nobody wants. Robert Hamrin discussed the syndrome of indiscriminate economic growth and especially the prospects for alternative concepts more in touch with contemporary political and social realities. Elizabeth Dodson Gray discussed the conceptual trap of the patriarchal society.

    Wilson's and Hamrin's positions are summarized in articles in *Making It Happen: A Positive Guide to the Future* published by USA/Club of Rome on the tenth anniversary of the publication of *The Limits to Growth* in March 1982 and also available through Roundtable Press. See also Robert Hamrin, *Managing Growth in the 1980s: Toward a New Economics* (New York: Praeger, 1980).

Chapter 1. Patriarchy

1. Margaret Mead, *Male and Female: A Study of the Sexes in a Changing World* (New York: Morrow Paperback, William Morrow & Co., 1949, 1975), pp. 159–160.
2. Michelle Zimbalist Rosaldo and Louise Lamphere, ed., *Woman, Culture, and Society* (Stanford, Calif.: Stanford University Press, 1974), pp. 3 and 70.
3. Elizabeth Janeway, *Between Myth and Morning: Women Awakening* (New York: William Morrow & Co., 1975), pp. 3–4.
4. Elizabeth Gould Davis, *The First Sex* (New York: Penguin Books, 1972).
5. Merlin Stone, *When God Was a Woman* (New York: Harcourt Brace, 1978).
6. Traces of that overturn of the gods as it was experienced within the Judeo-Christian tradition are present in the Bible and are a part of the religious heritage and mythology we know today. See the account of the great Deuteronomic Reform under King Josiah (2 Kg. 22–23) as well as the Book of Deuteronomy. See also the earlier efforts at reform, first under Gideon (Jg. 6–7), and then against King Ahab under Elijah and later Elisha (1 Kg. 16–22), and the massacre by Jehu of all of King Ahab's descendants (2 Kg. 10). See also Hos. 2:2–8 and Jer. 23:13–15.
7. See Rose E. Frisch and Janet W. McArthur, "Menstrual Cycles: Fatness as a Determinant of Minimum Weight for Height Necessary for Their Maintenance or Onset," *Science*, 185 (1974): 949–951. Also Rose E. Frisch, "Population, Food Intake, and Fertility," *Science*, 199 (1978): 22–30.
8. See Martha K. McClintock, "Menstrual Synchrony and Suppression," *Nature* 229 (1971): 244–245; and also Michael J. Russell, Genevieve M. Switz, and Kate Thompson, "Olfactory Influences on the Human Menstrual Cycle," *Pharmacology, Biochemistry and Behavior* 13 (1980): 737–738.
9. See Elise Boulding, *The Underside of History: A View of Women through Time* (Boulder, Colorado: Westview Press, 1976).
10. Michelle Zimbalist Rosaldo, "Woman, Culture, and Society: A Theoretical Overview," in *Woman, Culture, and Society*, ed. Rosaldo and Lamphere, pp. 23–24.

11. See Perdita Huston, *Third World Women Speak Out: Interviews in Six Countries on Change, Development, and Basic Needs* (New York: Praeger Publishers in cooperation with the Overseas Development Council, 1979). Also, *Message from the Village* (New York: The Epoch B Foundation, 1978).
12. Rosaldo, p. 24. Emphasis added.
13. Evelyn Reed, *Sexism and Science* (New York: Pathfinder Press, 1978).
14. Carl B. Koford, "Group Relations in an Island Colony of Rhesus Monkeys," in *Primate Social Behavior,* ed. Charles W. Southwick (New York: D. Van Nostrand Co., 1963), p. 149. Cited in Reed, p. 30.
15. S.L. Washburn and Irven DeVore, "The Social Life of Baboons" in *Primate Social Behavior, p. 108. Cited in Reed, p. 29.*
16. Reed, p. 30.
17. Mead, *Male and Female,* pp. 159–160. Emphasis added.

Chapter 2. The Social Construction of Reality

1. Peter L. Berger and Thomas Luckmann, *The Social Construction of Reality: A Treatise in the Sociology of Knowledge* (Garden City, N.Y.: Anchor Books, Doubleday, 1967).
2. Thomas S. Kuhn, *The Structure of Scientific Revolutions,* 2nd ed. (Chicago: University of Chicago Press, 1970).
3. Kuhn, pp. 115–117.
4. Fritjof Capra, *The Tao of Physics: An Exploration of the Parallels between Modern Physics and Eastern Mysticism* (Berkeley, Calif.: Shambhala Publications, 1975).
5. Ronald M. Green, *Religious Reason: The Rational and Moral Basis of Religious Belief* (New York: Oxford University Press, 1978).

Chapter 3. Patriarchy as a Social Construction of Reality

1. Lawrence Kohlberg and Richard Kramer, "Continuities and Discontinuities in Childhood and Adult Moral Development," *Human Development* 12 (1969): 93–120.
2. Carol Gilligan, "In a Different Voice: Women's Conception of the Self and of Morality," *Harvard Educational Review* 47 (1977): 481–517.
3. Carol Gilligan, *In a Different Voice: Essays on Psychological Theory and Women's Development* (Cambridge, Mass.: Harvard University Press, 1982).
4. Lawrence Kohlberg, *The Philosophy of Moral Development: Essays in Moral Development,* vol. 1 (New York: Harper and Row, 1981).
5. Nancy Chodorow, *The Reproduction of Mothering: Psychoanalysis and the Sociology of Gender* (Berkeley, Calif.: University of California Press, 1978).
6. This quotation is taken from the excellent condensed description of Chodorow's analysis, which appears in Lillian Breslow Rubin, *Worlds of Pain: Life in the Working-Class Family* (New York: Basic Books, 1976), pp. 118–119. "... Nancy Chodorow has presented us with a brilliant and provocative reformulation of Oedipal theory which successfully crosses the sociological with the psychological as it accounts for the dynamics of both the inner and outer world as they affect sex-role development.... For a girl, that task is a relatively straightforward one—a continuous and gradual process of internalization of a feminine identity with mother as model. For a boy, however, role learning is discontinuous involving, as it must, the rejection of his early identification with his mother as he seeks an appropriate masculine identity."
7. Gilligan article, "In a Different Voice," p. 509. See also Carol Gilligan, "Woman's Place in Man's Life Cycle," *Harvard Educational Review* 49 (1979): 431–446.
8. For an overview and critical assessment of recent research about "dual functional brain asymmetry," see Jeannette McGlone, "Sex Differences in Human Brain Asymmetry: A Critical Survey," *The Behavioral and Brain Sciences* 3(1980): 215–263. For a responsible journalistic presentation of some of this material, see Patricia McBroom, "Why Can't a Woman Think More Like a Man (And Vice Versa)?" *Today,* Philadelphia *Inquirer* magazine, 15 Feb. 1981.
9. The research reported by McBroom on the water-level of the glass was done by Dr. Lauren Jay Harris, Dept. of Psychology, Michigan State University. See his article in *Readings in Child Development and Relationships,* ed. Mollie Smart and Russell Smart (New York: Macmillan Co., 1977).

10. The research about contextual awareness—what psychologists have called "field dependence"—was reported by McBroom and based upon the writings and interpretations of Dr. Jerre Levy, a neurologist in the Dept. of Behavioral Sciences, University of Chicago.

11. Judith Plaskow, *Sex, Sin and Grace: Women's Experience and the Theologies of Reinhold Niebuhr and Paul Tillich* (Washington, D.C.: University Press of America, 1980).

12. Sheila G. Davaney, "The Idea of Divine Power in the Thought of Karl Barth and Charles Hartshorne: Its Foundations and Implications" (Ph.D. diss., Harvard University, 1981).

13. Elizabeth Dodson Gray, *Green Paradise Lost* (Wellesley, Mass.: Roundtable Press, 1981), p. 150.

14. Roger Kasperson, "Remarks," *Proceedings of Conference on Public Policy Issues in Nuclear Waste Management* (a conference supported by ERDA, NRC, NSF, CEQ and EPA through NSF Contract No. C-1044 with the MITRE Corporation of McLean, Virginia, October 27–29, 1976), p. 259. Also Elizabeth Dodson Gray, "Remarks," p. 201.

15. Margaret Hennig and Anne Jardim, *The Managerial Woman* (New York: Kangaroo Book, Pocket Books, 1978), pp. 47–50, pp. 209–210.

16. Laura Nader, "Barriers to Thinking New about Energy," *Physics Today* 34.2 (February 1981): 9.

17. Margaret Mead, comment to Amory Lovins in private conversation, cited by Lovins in his comment printed on the rear cover of *Green Paradise Lost,* by Gray.

18. Peter L. Berger, *The Sacred Canopy: Elements of a Sociological Theory of Religion* (Garden City, N.Y.: Doubleday and Co., 1967).

19. *Bradwell* v. *State of Illinois,* cited by *Time,* 20 July 1981, p. 17 as part of its cover story about President Reagan's nomination of Judge Sandra Day O'Connor to the Supreme Court.

Chapter 4. Imaging Our Place as Humans on Planet Earth

1. Walter Lippmann, *Public Opinion* (New York: Macmillan Co., 1922).

2. Gray, chapter 1.

See also Loren Eiseley, *Darwin's Century: Evolution and the Men Who Discovered It* (New York: Doubleday & Co., Anchor Books, 1958, 1961), pp. 5–10, the section "The Two Ladders and the Scale of Being." "Widespread in the literature of the seventeenth and eighteenth centuries, and easily traceable into earlier periods, is the theological doctrine known variously as the *Scala Naturae,* Chain of Being, *echelle des etre,* Ladder of Perfection, and by other similar titles."

Eiseley references A.O. Lovejoy's *The Great Chain of Being* (1942) and quotes Sir Thomas Browne in the *Religio Medici* (1635): "There is in this Universe a Stair, rising not disorderly, or in confusion, but with a comely method and proportion." And since the Scale of Nature runs from minerals by insensible degrees upward through the lower forms of life to man, and beyond him to purely spiritual existences like the angels, ourselves, compounded of both dust and spirit, become "that great and true Amphibium, whose nature is disposed to live. . . in divided and distinguished worlds." p. 7.

3. H. Paul Santmire, *Brother Earth: Nature, God and Ecology in Time of Crisis* (Camden, N.J.: Thomas Nelson, 1970).

4. See Charles Darwin, *The Illustrated Origin of Species,* abridged and introduced by Richard E. Leakey (1859; New York: Hill and Wang, 1979), *The Descent of Man and Selection in Relation to Sex* (1871), and *The Expression of the Emotions in Man and Animals* (1872). For a biographical reconstruction of Darwin's longstanding concern about the anticipated hostile reception of *The Origin of Species* and his original plans for publication only after his own death, see Irving Stone, *The Origin: A Biographical Novel of Charles Darwin* (New York: New American Library, Plume Book), p. 439 et passim.

5. The historical process of transition from what I have called mental picture number one to mental picture number two is recounted by Loren Eiseley in *Darwin's Century,* chapters 1 3.

6. J. Bronowski, *The Ascent of Man* (Boston, Mass.: Little, Brown, 1973).

7. Peter Morgane, "The Whale Brain: The Anatomical Basis of Intelligence," in *Mind in the Waters: A Book to Celebrate the Consciousness of Whales and Dolphins,* ed. Joan McIntyre (New York: Charles Scribner's Sons, 1974), pp. 84–93.

8. An excellent example of new learnings about what we have inadvertently done is the recent work of Dr.Jelle Atema, a marine biologist at Woods Hole (Massachusetts) Oceanographic Institution. He and his colleagues have discovered that the chemical communication necessary for lobsters to recognize the presence of food, and also to mate, is disrupted by 0.3 parts of drilling mud per million parts of water.

See Jelle Atema, Stewart Jacobson, Elisa Karnofsky, Susan Oleszkoszuts and Lauren Stein, "Pair Formation in the Lobster *Homarus Americanus:* Behavioral Development, Pheromones and Mating," in *Marine Behavior and Psychology* 1979:6(277-296). Also see Jelle Atema, Elisa Karnofsky, Susan Oleszkoszuts, "Lobster Behavior and Chemoreception: Sublethal Effects of #2 Fuel Oil," in *Advances in Marine Environmental Research,* ed. F.S. Jacoff, September 1977, pp. 122–134 (Washington, DC: U.S. Environmental Protection Agency, 1977—600/9-79-035).

A journalistic account can be found in "Will Georges Bank Lobsters Survive Drilling Mud?" by Matthew Douglas in Boston *Globe,* 16 October 1981. The principal investigator, Jelle Atema, has written a popular article, "A Sensible Mix of Lobsters and Oil," in *The World at Boston University,* 16 July 1981.

When I last talked with Dr. Atema, the funding for this research had recently been cancelled!
9. Dorothy Dinnerstein, *The Mermaid and the Minotaur: Sexual Arrangements and Human Malaise* (New York: Harper & Row, 1976), p. 95.
10. Gray, pp. 40–42.

Chapter 5. The Trap of Separation

1. Gray, ix.
2. Rubin, pp. 118–119.
3. Ernest Becker, *The Denial of Death* (New York: Free Press, Macmillan Co., 1973).
4. Carol P. Christ, *Diving Deep and Surfacing: Women Writers on Spiritual Quest* (Boston, Mass.: Beacon Press, 1980).
5. Carol P. Christ and Judith Plaskow, ed., *Womanspirit Rising: A Feminist Reader in Religion* (San Francisco, Calif.: Harper & Row, 1979).
6. Gray, chapter 15.

Chapter 6. Looking Ahead

1. See Joseph R. Strayer, *On the Medieval Origins of the Modern State* (Princeton, N.J.: Princeton University Press, 1970). "Personal loyalty to the ruler reached its peak in the doctrine of divine right. If only one man, clearly designated by God, had the right to rule a particular country at a given moment, then all right-thinking people ought to obey him without question. In earlier periods men could accept the idea that monarchy was the best form of government without believing that all commmands of a particular monarch had to be obeyed, or that any one monarch was irreplaceable. Acceptance of the theory of divine right monarchy made resistance illegitimate and so strengthened the state. For those who were sceptical about the divine right of monarchs there was the theory that the state was absolutely necessary for human welfare, and that that concentration of power which we call sovereignty was essential for the existence of the state. Men could not live a decent life—in fact, according to Hobbes[writing immediately after the restoration of the monarchy and following the Cromwellian Revolution] they could not live at all—unless they lived in and obeyed the commands of a sovereign state. To weaken or to destroy the state was to threaten the future of the human race. Therefore a state was entitled to take any steps to ensure its own survival, even if those steps seemed unjust or cruel" (pp.107–108).

Note the parallels with the assumed divine right of the human species to dominion (i.e., monarchy) and the similar derivative lines of reasoning.
2. Gray, ix.
3. Gray, p. 158.